KINGDOM

HOW ANDY REID, PATRICK MAHOMES, AND THE KANSAS CITY CHIEFS RETURNED TO SUPER BOWL GLORY

ADAM TEICHER

TRIUMPH
BOOKS

Library of Congress has catalogued the previous edition as follows:

Names: Teicher, Adam, author.
Title: Kingdom: how Andy Reid, Patrick Mahomes, and the Kansas City Chiefs returned to Super Bowl glory / Adam Teicher.
Description: Chicago, Illinois: Triumph Books, 2020. | Summary: "This book chronicles the Kansas City Chiefs' Super Bowl LIV-winning season"— Provided by publisher.
Identifiers: LCCN 2020022819 (print) | LCCN 2020022820 (ebook) | ISBN 9781629378558 (hardcover) | ISBN 9781641255530 (epub)
Subjects: LCSH: Kansas City Chiefs (Football team) | Super Bowl (54th: 2020 : Miami Gardens, Miami-Dade County, Fla.) | Reid, Andy, 1958- | Mahomes, Patrick, 1995-
Classification: LCC GV956.K35 T45 2020 (print) | LCC GV956.K35 (ebook) | DDC 796.332/6409778411—dc23
LC record available at https://lccn.loc.gov/2020022819
LC ebook record available at https://lccn.loc.gov/2020022820

This book is available in quantity at special discounts for your group or organization. For further information, contact:

Triumph Books LLC
814 North Franklin Street
Chicago, Illinois 60610
(312) 337-0747
www.triumphbooks.com

Printed in U.S.A.
ISBN: 978-1-63727-360-9
Design by Jonathan Hahn
Photos courtesy of AP Images

To my wife, Barbara, always my inspiration. To our daughter, Hannah, who is well on her way to conquering the world. To my mom and dad, who died way too early but will never be forgotten.

CONTENTS

FOREWORD

AS ONE OF THE COACHES who tried to get the Kansas City Chiefs to win a Super Bowl in between 1970 and 2020, nobody was happier to see them win it than I was. I know all the work that was put in by so many people for so many years to try to make it happen. No city deserved it more than Kansas City. I felt best for the Chiefs fans. Every team says it has the best fans. Every coach says that, every general manager says that, and every owner says that. But it's tough to beat the people in Kansas City. Those fans are so loyal and they're not quite as bitter when you lose. There's a little higher degree of compassion within the personality profile of Midwestern people. I also coached the Philadelphia Eagles and I love the Philadelphia fans, but the fans in Kansas City didn't get quite as mad when the team loses.

One of the first people I thought of when the Chiefs won the Super Bowl was Lamar Hunt. He founded the franchise and the old American Football League and, of course, passed away in 2006. He would have responded more humbly than any other owner in the history of winning a championship. I don't think there would be anybody happier for the right reasons, starting with the fans but also including the people in the organization and the people who used to play or work for the organization.

I have a number of disappointments and things I don't feel I did well enough in the course of my career. We all do. But not being able to hand Lamar Hunt the Lamar Hunt Trophy as we moved on into the Super Bowl was the biggest disappointment in regard to my career. So many great things happened, but the icing on the cake would have been handing him that trophy with his name on it. I was very fortunate to develop a personal relationship with Lamar and I know that he appreciated my five years there very much. He was very open about it. I don't know how many coaches can really say that about someone they worked for in the National Football League. I can imagine how much he would appreciate the job that Andy Reid and his staff did.

I never felt Lamar questioned or second-guessed my approach to coaching. In fact, he told me many times he appreciated my leadership style, which made me feel good about it. There was a lot of support from him, and now I have two beautiful letters from Clark Hunt, his son and the Chiefs' chairman since Lamar's death, saying the same thing. So Lamar obviously passed along his personal feelings within his family. I'm so happy for Clark that he hired Andy when he did, and that he's been as successful as he has with the Chiefs.

The Chiefs had some teams that were good enough to win the Super Bowl in between Super Bowl IV and Super Bowl LIV. Some of the teams that Marty Schottenheimer had in the 1990s were definitely good enough to win a Super Bowl. But unlike in Major League Baseball or the NBA, the playoffs are the best of one. One game eliminates you. There were a few times where his teams were good enough to get there and win it. They lost a lot of close games. They just couldn't get it done at the right time. I coached the Chiefs for five years. Our 2003 team, the only one of my teams to make the playoffs, wasn't quite good enough on defense to win a Super Bowl. We won the AFC West and got a first-round playoff bye, but we weren't strong enough on defense to beat the Indianapolis Colts.

The best thing the Chiefs ever did was hire Andy in 2013. I talked to him when Clark contacted him about coaching the Chiefs. He asked me, "What do you think?"

I said, "Take the job."

We were friends, and I had coached here for five years so I knew about the team and the organization. I told him it was a great place to work, that the Hunts were a great family to represent, that it was a great city to represent, and that it was a great city to live in. I think he was going to take the job anyway, but what I told him probably didn't hurt.

You can't buy Andy's experience. He's a humble guy and has a tremendous work ethic. The scheme he puts his quarterback in is extremely mature. He's been able to increase the horsepower in it every year since he's been with the Chiefs. He makes it better by eliminating this and adding that. He had all of these great players like Travis Kelce and Tyreek Hill and now he has a quarterback who has no limitation on what he can ask him to do. Those two—Reid and Patrick Mahomes—are a great match for one another.

I can't remember when I first met Andy, but I've always followed closely the coaches who replaced me with the Eagles and tried to be very supportive because I know how tough that job is. I do remember coaching against him, and it was always a challenge. My teams played against his three times and I never won. During my Super Bowl-winning season with the St. Louis Rams in 1999, we went up to Philadelphia for the last game of the regular season, and his team scored 38 points against us. Then we lost to him twice when I was with the Chiefs. We had a good team in 2005 and had a 24–6 lead against them late in the first half. Then his quarterback, Donovan McNabb, threw three touchdown passes, and they came back to beat us. Andy's team is never out of a game. You saw that in 2019 when they were down 24 points in their first playoff game, 10 points in their second playoff game, and then 10 points in the fourth quarter of the Super Bowl, and they won each time. On his gameplan card—I know this because I've sat in on his offensive gameplan and quarterback meetings—there's something there for every situation. And then you can throw in Andy's years of experience of when and how to use it. That part of it is important, too, and he's exceptional with that.

The thing about Andy as a coach that strikes you is how he keeps his emotions on an even plane. To be able to go through all the highs and lows that he's gone through all these years and still retain the same passion is remarkable. Coaching in the NFL is very difficult. That's why I got out of it for 15 years after I left the Eagles. I can tell you better than anybody the toll it takes on you. Andy handles that better or as well as any coach I've ever seen. I really admire him for that. Another thing that sets him apart is that he's got great intellectual humility. He's not afraid to say, "I don't know what I don't know" and then ask somebody on his staff for help with that. Then, of course, Andy is the first one to give that coach the credit.

The Chiefs were good enough in 2018 to win a Super Bowl. They probably should have won it that year. Then you look at the things that happened in 2019. The New England Patriots were not the same team as the year before. The Baltimore Ravens may have been the best team in the NFL, but they got knocked out of the playoffs before the Chiefs had to play them. The Chiefs' big offseason moves—where they signed safety Tyrann Mathieu and traded for defensive end Frank Clark—worked out well. All of those things don't happen every year. So you had a feeling this might be their season. I started to wonder a little bit in the middle of the season when they hit a rough patch, but they came out of it just fine, and you had the feeling when the regular season ended that it was going to be their year.

I came to a Chiefs game late in the season. They played the Denver Broncos at Arrowhead Stadium so I came in a couple of days early. Andy invited me to talk to the team. I went to a team meeting, an offensive meeting, the quarterback meeting, and practice. So I got a pretty good behind-the-scenes look at the operation. No one's doing it any better than Andy does it.

The Chiefs in 2019 were a fun team to watch. I try to watch as much NFL as I can and I'll go back and watch film of the games I can't get to live. I tried not to miss any of the Chiefs because they had so many good players and were so well-coached. Mahomes will end up being the next Tom Brady in terms of how many championships he wins because he's got Andy. Tom Brady doesn't win all of those championships without Bill Belichick, and Belichick doesn't win all of those without Brady. Andy never had a Brady, but he has one now.

—*Dick Vermeil*
Philadelphia Eagles head coach (1976–82)
St. Louis Rams head coach (1997–99)
Kansas City Chiefs head coach (2001–05)

INTRODUCTION

WHEN I WAS FIRST APPROACHED by the editors at Triumph Books about writing this book, I was enthusiastic about the idea. The stories of the 2019 Kansas City Chiefs were too rich not to be told. The emotions of the season—from the despair of the Patrick Mahomes injury and later what looked like a devastating loss to the Tennessee Titans to the highs of Super Bowl LIV and really the last several games—had too much range to be ignored.

But the book also gave me a chance to dig a little bit into the previous 50 years since the Chiefs last won a Super Bowl in 1970. That's essential to the story of the 2019 Chiefs. Every team without a Super Bowl title for so long has a tortured history to tell, but the Chiefs' has its own particular flavor. They were close a few times but could never seem to get out of their own way when it counted the most. Their inability—more of a refusal, really—for most of their history to go out and get a quarterback to call their own was almost criminal, particularly when considering the results the first time the Chiefs ever went all in on a quarterback they had drafted.

The seeming ease with which it all happened makes me wonder how many championships the Chiefs would have won in those 50 years had they earlier worked to find a quarterback and then committed to him, as they finally did with Mahomes.

The probable answer, though, is none. The Chiefs by 2019 had the right coach for their quarterback in Andy Reid, one who not only was unafraid of playing a young quarterback, but also embraced the idea. Chiefs history is very short on coaches like that. The 2019 Chiefs were also the most complete team the franchise had in at least 50 years. They were known for Mahomes and a high-scoring offense but were capable of winning with their defense, as they showed at times later in the season.

So 2019 was just the right time—for the Chiefs to win a Super Bowl and for me to write this book. I've been covering the Chiefs on a daily basis since 1993 first for *The Kansas City Star* and the last seven years for ESPN. After seeing good coaches like Marty Schottenheimer and Dick Vermeil fail to get the Chiefs to a Super Bowl, I started to think that maybe I wasn't going to be around long enough to see it happen. I became convinced of that during the darkest of times for the Chiefs in the late 2000s and early 2010s, when the Chiefs were lost and didn't seem to know the way out.

I was okay with that. Like most writers covering a team, I was in it more for the stories and the people than the winning and losing. The 2019 Chiefs, however, provided not only the Super Bowl championship, but also an abundance of stories—enough to fill this book.

With Reid as their coach and Mahomes as their quarterback, the Chiefs may go on a run of Super Bowl championships. That's a reasonable assumption given all the franchise has going for it. But it's also logical they will never have a season like the one in 2019, one that started with plenty of anticipation and decades of pent-up demand and ended in spectacular comeback fashion.

1

A 50-YEAR WAIT

HUNDREDS OF THOUSANDS OF FANS turned out in sub-freezing tempera-tures in February of 2020 for the parade and rally to celebrate the Kansas City Chiefs' victory against the San Francisco 49ers in Super Bowl LIV. A handful of players and team officials spoke, but it was left to Travis Kelce to sum up the day in the most eloquent of terms. "This is,'" said the Chiefs' tight end, who caught a fourth-quarter touchdown pass to help his team rally from a 10-point deficit to claim a 31–20 victory, "the most beautiful scene I've ever witnessed in my life."

Judging by the screams he drew from fans, it wasn't the most popu-lar of the comments Kelce made that day. Among others—his opening line of "Can you dig it?" and later when he twice bellowed, "You've got to fight for your right to party!"—elicited stronger reactions. The latter—first shouted by Kelce in the on-field celebration immediately after the Chiefs won the AFC Championship Game—was borrowed from the Beastie Boys song of the same title. It quickly became an anthem of sorts for Chiefs fans in Kansas City and elsewhere.

But many Chiefs fans and particularly those under 50 years old could agree with Kelce's statement about the scene that cold February day outside Kansas City's Union Station. The under-50 crowd wasn't around the last time the Chiefs held a Super Bowl victory parade in 1970.

It was a long, hard 50 years for the franchise and its fans. Several teams won multiple Super Bowl championships in the half-century. The New England Patriots and Pittsburgh Steelers each had six titles since 1970. The Dallas Cowboys and 49ers had five apiece. The New York Giants won four times, three teams had three titles, and four others were two-time champions. The Chiefs not only couldn't win a championship in those 50 years, but also failed to even get to a Super Bowl and lose. Seldom were they even close. They advanced as far as the AFC Championship Game only twice in the half-century.

It was always something holding the Chiefs back. Whether it was lousy drafting, a refusal to find and commit to a franchise quarterback, poor choices in coaching, or sometimes just bad luck, the Chiefs could never in 50 years get it right.

They were winners in their first 10 seasons—the first three spent in Dallas, where they were known as the Texans—and as members of the old American Football League. The franchise moved to Kansas City and was renamed the Chiefs in 1963. The Texans/Chiefs won three AFL titles. They overcame the infamous "kick to the clock" in the 1962 AFL title game when their captain, calling the overtime coin flip, uttered those words after the coin toss went the Texans' way. The Texans wound up not only starting the extra period on defense, but also going into the wind as well. They ultimately prevailed anyway.

The Chiefs played in Super Bowl I, losing to the Green Bay Packers. They later won Super Bowl IV 23–7 against the Minnesota Vikings. The Chiefs allowed a total of 20 points in their three postseason games following the 1969 season, and with eight players and coach Hank Stram, who would eventually wind up in the Pro Football Hall of Fame, Kansas City looked like it might be ready to start a dynasty. With a Hall of Fame coach and so many talented players, why didn't those Chiefs go on a championship run? "We've been wondering about that for 50 years," said former Chiefs cornerback Emmitt Thomas, one of those nine Hall of Famers. "We sit around as old men now and wonder about that."

It took another 50 years and a heaping dose of heartache for the franchise and its fans before the Chiefs would get back to the Super Bowl again. Two years after winning Super Bowl IV, they reached the playoffs again after the 1971 season. But they lost in the playoffs in what remains the longest NFL game ever played. Kicker Jan Stenerud, one of those nine eventual Hall of Famers from that earlier Super Bowl champion team, missed three field goals, and the Chiefs were beaten by the Miami Dolphins.

From there the Chiefs aged quickly and didn't draft well enough to adequately replace their many future Hall of Fame players. It was another 15 seasons before the Chiefs reached the playoffs again, and even then they floundered in a lopsided loss to the New York Jets in a wild-card round game.

In the 1990s the Chiefs had their best chance since 1970 to reach the Super Bowl under general manager Carl Peterson and coach Marty Schottenheimer. They reached the playoffs seven times in an eight-year period, winning the AFC West three times. But the Chiefs could rarely muster enough offense in the playoffs to advance very far. They lost playoff games in those seasons by scoring 16, 14, zero, 13, 17, seven, and 10 points. The Chiefs did score enough to win a couple of playoff games, following the 1993 season, to advance to the AFC Championship Game. But again they were barely competitive in a loss, and this one came against the Buffalo Bills.

Few teams had such a tortured playoff history as the Chiefs endured for 50 years. The 1971 playoff loss to the Dolphins was in that sense a scene-setter for what was to come. The Chiefs that day played more than 80 minutes of football, turned the game over to one of the NFL's all-time great kickers, and still couldn't get the job done.

In 1990 the Chiefs were driving to what would have been the winning field goal in the final moments of a wild-card round playoff game against the Dolphins. But a holding penalty on a running play pushed them back, and Nick Lowery, another one of the game's all-time great kickers, fell just short on a 52-yard attempt with 49 seconds left. The Chiefs lost 17–16.

In 1995 more field-goal failures ended the season for the best Chiefs' team since their Super Bowl victory. Late in that regular season, kicker Lin Elliott went into a slump, but the Chiefs failed to make a change. In a divisional round playoff game against the Indianapolis Colts, Elliott missed three field goal attempts. The last went horribly wide left from 42 yards with 37 seconds remaining, and the Chiefs lost 10–7.

Two years later the Chiefs had their kicking problems solved. They finished the regular season with an NFL best 13–3 record. But it was their bad luck in their playoff game to run into perhaps the league's second-best team, the Denver Broncos. Indeed, the game was tightly played. Every snap seemed like it might determine the outcome. The Chiefs appeared to have made one such game-changing play early in the third quarter on a touchdown pass from Elvis Grbac to Tony

Gonzalez. But officials ruled Gonzalez landed out of the end zone, and the Chiefs had nowhere to appeal in those pre-replay review days. They settled for a field goal, but those extra four points would have come in handy. They lost 14–10 to the Broncos, who went on to win the Super Bowl. To this day, Gonzalez will tell you he scored the touchdown and that the Chiefs were robbed.

The Chiefs eventually changed coaches from Schottenheimer to Dick Vermeil, but their postseason fortunes never changed. In 2003 Vermeil's Chiefs lost to Peyton Manning and the Colts 38–31 in a game, in which the Chiefs never even forced the Colts to punt. Things took a turn a decade later to the same team, and this loss to the Colts was even more cruel to the Chiefs. The Chiefs were cruising to a victory in the wild-card around in 2013 when they led the Colts 38–10 in the third quarter. Then they allowed Indianapolis to score five touchdowns on its final six possessions. The Chiefs lost 45–44.

In a divisional round game against the Steelers in 2016, they had what would have been a tying two-point conversion in the final minutes erased by a penalty. The Chiefs failed to score on their second try and lost 18–16, even though Pittsburgh never scored a touchdown. The following season the Chiefs were in control at halftime of a wild-card round game against the Tennessee Titans, leading 21–3. The Titans rallied for 19 second-half points while the Chiefs were shut out. They lost 22–21.

After advancing to the AFC Championship Game for the first time in 25 years in 2018, the Chiefs held a lead late in the fourth quarter against the Patriots and appeared to make the play that would send them back at long last to the Super Bowl. Cornerback Charvarius Ward intercepted a Tom Brady pass, which would have allowed the

Chiefs to merely run out the clock. But the Chiefs had a player, Dee Ford, who lined up offside, and the Patriots retained the ball. They went on to score and eventually win the game in overtime.

The Chiefs' best teams of the half-century without a Super Bowl were often in fact half a team. The Chiefs frequently had championship quality defensive teams during the 1990s, featuring top pass rushers like Derrick Thomas and Neil Smith. But the offense often couldn't carry its fair share of the load, particularly against stronger opponents in the playoffs. The Chiefs of the early 2000s featured a high-scoring offense with players like running back Priest Holmes and Gonzalez. But those teams mostly struggled because of a poor defense.

Kansas City's 50 years of futility were best illustrated by the team's approach at quarterback. The Chiefs mostly left the game's most important position in the hands of someone at least one other team had found deficient. Even Hall of Famer Len Dawson, who quarterbacked all three of Kansas City's AFL title teams, including the 1970 Super Bowl winner, washed out with two teams before he joined the Chiefs.

Three times in the franchise's first 57 years, the Chiefs drafted a quarterback in the first round: Pete Beathard in 1964, Steve Fuller in 1979, and Todd Blackledge in 1983. Even then the Chiefs never made much a commitment to any of them. Beathard made just two starts for the Chiefs in three seasons. Fuller lasted four seasons in Kansas City, and Blackledge lasted five, but they were rarely more than intermittent starters. Fuller started 31 games, and Blackledge started 24. The combined record of the three players was 29–33.

The Chiefs would occasionally try to win with one of their lower-round draft picks at quarterback, but they mostly went with a succession of veterans, who for one reason or another were rejected by other teams. This list included an aging and end-of-his-career Joe Montana, who had been ousted by the 49ers by Steve Young and then traded to Kansas City, where he played two seasons before retiring.

From 1984 through 2016, the Chiefs did not select a quarterback in the first round of the draft. The New Orleans Saints, who had their own dismal history, were the only other team to not draft a quarterback in the first round during that period. The Chiefs' fortune with quarterbacks and the draft is such that the one time in the last several years when they were in position to take a true franchise passer—in 2013, when the Chiefs had the first overall pick—none was available. This was just one year after the Colts selected a can't-miss quarterback, Andrew Luck, with the draft's top pick.

Even when the Chiefs tried, they got it wrong. In selecting Blackledge with the seventh overall pick in 1983, the Chiefs passed on two eventual Hall of Fame quarterbacks: Jim Kelly and Dan Marino. Blackledge threw 32 interceptions and 26 touchdown passes for the Chiefs.

Mostly, the Chiefs just never had the stomach to live with inevitable ups and downs of developing and playing a young quarterback, no matter how talented. "We tried on a couple of occasions to go with a second-round quarterback," said Peterson, the Chiefs' general manager from 1989 through 2008. "Neither one of them worked out. After the second one, I said, 'You know what? If I'm going to give up a first-round choice for a quarterback, I'm going to get one that I know about, that has a track record.' Most of the time we were drafting mid-to-late-first round. So you're not going to get a franchise quarterback. Even so, I felt if you had a high first-round draft choice, you would be better served to go either in another direction or trade down and get some extra choices and then you could spend it on a veteran quarterback—an accomplished, experienced, playoff-type quarterback—so at least you know what you're working with."

This dubious strategy left the Chiefs with this list of mostly undistinguished starting quarterbacks from Dawson's retirement in 1975 through 2016: Mike Livingston, Tony Adams, Fuller, Bill Kenney, Blackledge, Matt Stevens, Doug Hudson, Frank Seurer, Steve DeBerg, Ron Jaworski, Steve Pelluer, Mark Vlasic, Dave Krieg, Montana, Steve Bono, Rich Gannon, Grbac, Warren Moon, Trent Green, Damon Huard, Brodie Croyle, Tyler Thigpen, Matt Cassel, Tyler Palko, Kyle Orton, Brady Quinn, Alex Smith, Chase Daniel, and Nick Foles.

The Chiefs were serious about drafting a quarterback in the first round a few times over the years since they picked Blackledge in 1983. In 2001 Drew Brees was high on their draft board. "We went to Purdue to work him out," Peterson said. "He threw every ball perfectly. You'd put him up on the board, and he would wow you with his quick analysis."

The Chiefs instead traded their first-round pick shortly before the draft to the St. Louis Rams for Green, who wound up giving them six good seasons. But his career wasn't like that of Brees, who that year was taken by the San Diego Chargers with the first pick of the second round. In 2002 the Chiefs might have drafted Oregon's Joey Harrington. He went with the third overall pick to the Detroit Lions, three spots ahead of where the Chiefs drafted. "We certainly would have given it the full 15 minutes," Peterson said when asked what the

Chiefs would have done if Harrington was still on the board when they picked. "We liked him very much."

Harrington went on to have a disappointing career, but things might have worked out differently for him with the Chiefs, who in the early 2000s had one of the league's strongest offensive teams.

In 2008 the Chiefs were coached by Herm Edwards, who was willing to tolerate the ups and downs of playing a young quarterback. They would have drafted Matt Ryan of Boston College if the Atlanta Falcons hadn't taken him third overall—two spots ahead of the Chiefs. "Matt Ryan would have been the guy," Edwards said. "You knew he was going to be a great player in our league. We just couldn't get him. Atlanta had the pick, and they weren't going to move out of that pick."

The Chiefs had a good draft in 2008 without Ryan. They got a handful of players, who became key contributors to their AFC West-winning team in 2010. But they didn't get their franchise quarterback. "That's the problem," Edwards said. "We ended up getting some good players, but none of them played the quarterback position."

Given their struggles in finding a quarterback, it's no wonder they went so long without reaching the Super Bowl. The situation bottomed out for the Chiefs in 2012. They finished 2–14 and for the first time in franchise history had the dubious honor of picking first in the next year's draft. The season was punctuated late in the year when one of their players, linebacker Jovan Belcher, killed his girlfriend and then drove to the parking lot of the team's practice facility, where he committed suicide.

The Chiefs cleaned out their football department at the end of the season, and that's when the team's football fortunes started to change. They hired Andy Reid, the coach of the Philadelphia Eagles for 14 seasons before being let go at the end of the 2012 season, as their head coach. Reid made the playoffs 10 times in Philadelphia, though the Eagles made the Super Bowl just once and lost to the Patriots in that lone appearance. The Chiefs lacked any coherent sense of direction for years before hiring Reid, who immediately set the franchise on its upward course. He pushed the Chiefs to trade for Smith, a veteran quarterback who had once been the first overall pick of the draft by the 49ers.

Reid guided a team that finished 2–14 the previous season to a 9–0 start in 2013. That team wound up in the playoffs, the first of Reid's six postseason appearances in seven years with the Chiefs. The Chiefs are on a franchise-record streak of four consecutive AFC West titles. The Chiefs had never before even won two straight division titles. Reid also brought a sense of professionalism to an organization that had long searched for it. He built a solid coaching staff and had a succession plan in place when the Chiefs lost offensive coordinators Doug Pederson in 2016 and Matt Nagy in 2018. Both left for head coaching jobs elsewhere in the NFL, but the Chiefs moved on without missing a beat each time.

The hiring of Reid was but one factor in the Chiefs' seven-year march from 2–14 to Super Bowl champions. There were other primary reasons, including trading for Smith in 2013. Smith was sent to the Washington Redskins in 2018 and wasn't around to participate in the Chiefs' first Super Bowl in 50 years.

By the measure that counts the most, Smith failed in his five seasons with the Chiefs. He couldn't get a talented and well-coached team to the Super Bowl despite four trips to the playoffs, and as the starting quarterback, that's on his record. By every other gauge, Smith was a success. Smith stabilized what had been a shaky position for the Chiefs. Prior to his arrival in 2013, seven different players started at least one game for them at quarterback over the previous six seasons.

He also guided a forlorn franchise, one that had lost at least 12 games in four of the six seasons before he walked in the door, to the postseason four times. The Chiefs also won the AFC West in Smith's final two seasons, marking the first time in franchise history they won division titles in back-to-back years.

The Chiefs couldn't do much with those opportunities. They were 1–4 with Smith in the playoffs, and their four losses came by one, seven, two, and one points. They scored just 16 points in their postseason loss to the Steelers in 2016 and were shut out in the second half of their postseason defeat to the Titans the following season. Those failures were in large part why the Chiefs traded up in 2017 in the first round to draft Patrick Mahomes and why the Chiefs sent Smith to Washington.

Turn back the clock to 2013, though, and the Chiefs would have happily accepted then what Smith delivered. After six seasons of Huard, Croyle, Thigpen, Cassel, Palko, Orton, and Quinn, the Chiefs were in desperate need of a quarterback who could help them win games. Smith did that. He won 50 of his 76 starts in Kansas City for a team that had won 24 of its previous 76 games before he arrived. Smith threw 102 touchdown passes with 33 interceptions for the Chiefs, making him one of three quarterbacks with 100-plus touchdown passes and fewer than 40 interceptions in those five years. The others were Brady and Aaron Rodgers.

From a 2013 perspective, that was great stuff. From a 2018 vantage point, it was no longer enough. With plenty of help from Smith, the

Chiefs had raised the bar. They would no longer settle for what they would have five years ago. That's Smith's Kansas City legacy. For that, the Chiefs owe their former starting quarterback a debt of gratitude. "Alex is going to go down as one of my all-time favorite guys, players, and human beings, and everything else," Reid said after Smith was traded. "He set all these records here. But life in the National Football League is this: change takes place. We're fortunate to have [Mahomes] as the change. Not every team can say that. He's going to put his own mark on this thing, but that's in the future here. I don't have anything where I can stand up and say he's [going to] set a bunch of records. He hasn't done that yet. But we're very optimistic about it. It's an exciting time."

Perhaps his lasting legacy is the way he treated Mahomes, who was groomed from his arrival as a first-round pick in 2017 to eventually take Smith's job. Smith looked at Mahomes not as a rival but as a teammate. He helped Mahomes learn how to watch video, prepare every day as a starting quarterback, be a pro, and what to look for in opposing defenses. "I told Patrick that he could buy [Smith] a castle, and it wouldn't pay for the experience that he was able to have working with Alex in his introduction into the National Football League," Reid said.

Then there was the drafting Mahomes in 2017. The Chiefs' attitude toward drafting and developing a passer changed with the hiring of Reid, who succeeded earlier in his career with young Eagles quarterback Donovan McNabb. He didn't fear playing with an inexperienced player—as long as it was the right one. "I'm big on trusting the process," Reid said before the 2017 draft. "You sort it out, then you go get it, and then you go to work. Are you going to be right every time? No [but] you surely can't be passive or you're not going to get anywhere."

From there, it was a matter of timing and finding the right quarterback. The two converged in time for the 2017 draft. The Chiefs were 1–3 in the playoffs in Smith's first four seasons in Kansas City. The feeling was that the Chiefs had gone about as far as they could with him as their quarterback. By coincidence, the Chiefs identified the quarterback they felt was the top prospect to come along in years, and he would be available in that year's draft. That draft included two other top quarterback prospects in North Carolina's Mitch Trubisky and Clemson's Deshaun Watson. The Chiefs had a different favorite, one they had their eye on for some time.

Texas Tech's Mahomes had a strong and accurate arm. He had a knack for making successful off-schedule throws and played the game with a flair few others possessed. The Chiefs had all of the quarterbacks at their headquarters in Kansas City before the draft. Among other things, they showed video of plays and tested each player's vision and recall by asking them to diagram what they had seen on a whiteboard.

During that process for Mahomes, personnel director Brett Veach wandered by Reid's office. When Mahomes wasn't looking, Reid gave him the thumbs-up sign, an indication that Mahomes was passing a final test for the Chiefs to draft him. "We drew up a ton of plays, and they really tested my knowledge," Mahomes said. "I feel like I did well. I feel like I drew them up really well and explained them, explained what I did at Texas Tech and how it would relate and how different we were with how Coach Kingsbury let me really take control of that offense at Texas Tech. I feel like it went really well, and we got along great. It felt like a great relationship already."

The Chiefs had the 27th pick in the draft. Mahomes wouldn't be available when that pick rolled around. The Chiefs knew of interest in Mahomes by a handful of teams, including the Saints, Arizona Cardinals, and Giants. John Dorsey, then the Chiefs' general manager, read the draft perfectly. He positioned the Chiefs ahead of all of those teams and others by sending the 27th pick plus a first-round pick in 2018 to the Buffalo Bills for the 10th overall choice. Then the Chiefs completed the trade that would eventually make them Super Bowl champions by drafting Mahomes. "I felt to get this player, I had to be at 10," Dorsey said. "I know there were three teams that wanted this player very badly…This is a really good football player. I think these types of guys don't come around that often. I'm willing to invest in that type of player because I believe in his skillset and what he's going to develop into. This is a quarterback-driven league…You have to have these quarterbacks to succeed in the National Football League."

By the time the Chiefs drafted, Trubisky had already been selected by the Chicago Bears. But the Chiefs could have had Watson, who was drafted two picks later by the Houston Texans.

They had their hearts set on Mahomes. "We think they're both really good football players," Reid said at the time. "We just thought with what we do that Mahomes would fit in well. We had all the guys in. All the quarterbacks came in. We had an opportunity to spend six hours with each guy, and that was a great experience to have a chance to meet all the guys. Both those young men are tremendous young men…Everybody liked this guy. We couldn't find anybody that didn't like him. We got to know the kid before we got to know the kid. Everybody kind of just fell in love with the kid and what he was all about, and how he went about his business, and how he played. That doesn't happen every year. I'm saying it like it's easy. That's not something that happens every year. When that happens, [former Green Bay Packers general manager] Ron Wolf told me this a long time ago, 'If you have one of those guys that you like, you go get them.'"

Mahomes, who played in the spread offense in college, had plenty to learn about the NFL game. He had to learn things as basic as calling a play in a huddle, something he wasn't asked to do at Texas Tech. Some of his technique, including his footwork, needed plenty of refinement.

He was far from a finished product when he arrived in Kansas City, but he joined a willing and experienced tutor in Reid and perhaps the perfect one for him.

Earlier in his career, Reid had shown a nice touch with young quarterbacks such as Brett Favre, when he was an assistant with the Green Bay Packers, and McNabb, when he coached the Eagles. "I was a better player because of Andy Reid," McNabb said. "Andy's worked with a lot of quarterbacks, but the thing that's important is that they all have different styles. Myself, Brett Favre with the Green Bay Packers, he changed Alex Smith's career in Kansas City. Then there were a lot of young guys he had with the Eagles—even an older player like Michael Vick. He was really able to show Mike how to play the game. If he had him early in his career, he would have been a different type of Michael Vick. Mike would have been a great quarterback that way. Mike told me one time he wished he'd had Andy for his coach his whole career. He has the ability to work with different types of quarterbacks. He's going to build around his quarterback and create his offense around his talent. With Andy it's not what's worked for him when he's had different players over the years. It's what will work with the quarterback he has now."

McNabb became a starter midway through his rookie season. He wound up playing 11 seasons for Reid and was selected to play in the Pro Bowl six times. He recalled a play from his rookie season that illustrated how Reid tutored him into becoming a more aware quarterback. "I went to the line and was reading the defense and I could see a corner was all over my No. 1 read," McNabb said. "I remember thinking that it was going to be on me to make a play. I made a couple of pass rushers miss and kind of scrambled around, threw a deep ball down the field. Andy came back and said, 'Hey, that was a great play, but that's not what we're trying to do here.' For a young guy, I thought I just made a miraculous play, something I used to do in college. But then we went back later and analyzed the play, Andy showed me there were two guys open on the play: the No. 2 and No. 3 receivers in the progression. What he was telling me was not to feel like I had to make every play. He was telling me there would be opportunities for me in the offense if every receiver and running back was guarded. That will happen to [Mahomes]. He'll make a great play and he'll high-five with teammates, and they'll be excited, but then he'll go back and watch the film and see he missed the No. 2 and the No. 3 reads. Andy will have something to say to him about that."

Reid wasted little time in starting his work with Mahomes. He hired as an assistant coach Mike Kafka, a backup quarterback for a short time for Reid with the Eagles. Much of Kafka's job that first season was to work with Mahomes, but Reid was also hands-on. "It is extremely exciting," Mahomes said of working with Reid. "He's a coach you know is going to coach you well and you know is going to get the best out of you. You can come in every single day, knowing he is going to push you and make you the best quarterback you can possibly be...It speaks for itself. You watch guys that he's been with: Brett Favre, Donovan McNabb, just to name a few, guys that just really developed and became great quarterbacks in the league. It's a coach you want to be with."

The Chiefs would have to wait for their payoff on Mahomes. They remained committed to Smith as their starting quarterback for 2017, so Mahomes was a backup his rookie season. But they were willing to wait. While doing so, they eagerly anticipated what was to come. "Right now, Patrick is not absolutely ready to play," Reid said shortly after Mahomes was drafted. "He's got some work to do, but he's coming into a great room. He gets an opportunity to learn from Alex Smith, which will be a phenomenal experience for him, and learn the offense. So we have to be patient with him. Definitely not a finished product right now, but he has tremendous upside. We think he'll fit into this offense very well. He's a good person. He's intelligent. He's got great skill, and I just think he'll be a great Kansas City Chief when it's all said and done."

Mahomes' first chance to start came in the final regular-season game of 2017 because the Chiefs rested several starters after clinching their playoff seed. Late in the fourth quarter of a tie game against the Broncos, Mahomes led the winning drive by completing four passes for 52 yards and converting twice on third downs. It was only a peek, but to those paying attention, the football world could see what was to come. "I like the way he went about business," Reid said. "We were able to take him and lead him into that game throughout the whole week…What that did was it allowed you to get a feel for him for down the road, whenever that time was, and I liked what I saw and felt there. I think he handled things very well, prepared to the T on that, handled himself very well. I came out of that going, 'You know what? This kid is ready to go. He's ready to go ahead and lead.'"

The decision to part with Smith and make Mahomes the starting quarterback at the end of the 2017 season was a remarkably simple one for the Chiefs. Smith responded to Mahomes' arrival with the best season of his career. He was the NFL's top-rated passer (104.7) and set personal records for yards (4,042) and touchdowns (26). But that didn't change the dynamics of the quarterback situation in Kansas City. Mahomes' promotion into the starting lineup was always going to be about him and when he had shown Reid and the Chiefs enough to where they felt comfortable he was ready.

The Chiefs had denied their future at quarterback for almost 50 years and couldn't afford to wait another day. So all Smith's big 2017 season accomplished was to fatten the return that the Chiefs could get for him in a trade. The Chiefs sent Smith to Washington for a draft pick and a defensive back, Kendall Fuller, who went on to make the interception that ended San Francisco's final possession in Super Bowl LIV.

Mahomes was an immediate success, throwing four touchdown passes in the 2018 season opener against the Los Angeles Chargers and six the following week against the Steelers. He finished the season as the second player in NFL history to throw 50 touchdown passes and for more than 5,000 yards. In his first try, he was the NFL's Most Valuable Player.

"You knew it was inevitable, it was coming," Veach said when asked whether Mahomes' debut season was at all a surprise. "I would say the thing that surprised me was the ease at which he did it, the consistency at which he did it. Even with the great players who are young, I think you always anticipate maybe [hitting] a wall. At some point after seven or eight weeks, opposing defenses figure this kid out. They throw a couple of different looks, coverages, or combinations that give him issues, but there was never really any issues. There was never really a time where that happened."

Reid, meanwhile, was energized by being able to work with a young quarterback as talented as Mahomes. The Chiefs held a party for their season-ticket holders shortly before the start of training camp in 2018, Mahomes' first season as the starting quarterback, and the gathering turned into an impromptu pep rally when Reid stepped forward to speak. Firing up the masses is generally not Reid's way. He's usually even-keeled to the point that sometimes after a game it's difficult to tell from his demeanor whether the Chiefs won or lost. But because of Mahomes, this would be no ordinary season for Reid or the Chiefs. "He's more excited than I've seen him in a long time," said Chiefs president Mark Donovan, who had worked with Reid for the past five years in Kansas City and before that with the Eagles. "The excitement that was in that room is something that matters. It's different. You feel it."

This sense about Reid extends beyond those who work with him on a daily basis. "I know he's excited about the team he has," said McNabb, who stays in contact with his former coach. "He liked Alex

Smith. He led them to the AFC West championship and also the playoffs, but there's something about having a young quarterback with potential. Patrick Mahomes can make off-schedule plays. That's a dimension to the offense that Andy hasn't had in a while."

Even Reid acknowledged that he has a different sense of anticipation about that season. Reid spoke to the change not only at quarterback, but also elsewhere on the Chiefs' roster. "There's more new on both sides of the ball," he said. "Some of the old guys, that have been here, aren't here. Whether it's the quarterback position, the inside linebacker position, the outside linebacker position, you're missing a few of those guys and you have new guys coming in that you have an opportunity to see perform. Some of them we haven't seen. That's exciting to me. I'm looking forward to that."

Reid wouldn't be pinned down to the idea that his excitement was tied to having Mahomes as his quarterback. A big fan of Smith's, he was fearful anything he said could come off as disrespect to his former quarterback. Others would say it for him, though. "There are some concepts and throws that Pat is really built for: deep overs and all that kind of stuff," Veach said. "Back in Philadelphia when we had DeSean [Jackson] and Jeremy [Maclin], we used to go just bombs away. You saw a little bit more of that last year, but over the years, he really pulled back on those kind of play concepts because it wasn't really to Alex's strengths. Coach is a very aggressive playcaller, and there are certain concepts that he feels like—with some of the speed we have now with Sammy and Tyreek and then the arm strength Pat has—he gets a little excited thinking about the possibilities."

As much as anything, Reid enjoys the teaching part of his job. Mahomes had plenty to learn to become an NFL-ready quarterback.

"He was always teaching," said Kafka, who was promoted to quarterbacks coach in 2018. "Every single play presents something new and is an opportunity to get better, whether that's with footwork, ball placement, accuracy, ballhandling. There are always the little things to focus on and work on. Andy stresses that on every play, no matter if it's a completion or an incompletion, a touchdown or an interception. There was always something better you could have done on every play. He takes that mentality into the quarterback room no matter who the players are."

In Mahomes, he had an eager pupil. A baseball player of note when he was younger, Mahomes was late getting into football. He started 29 games at Texas Tech but played in the spread offense, leaving him much to learn about an NFL passing game.

Reid liked Mahomes' desire to learn and capacity to process the information. "I've been lucky to have been around some Hall of Fame players," Reid said. "The one thing they wanted you to do as a coach is to give them one more thing to make them even greater than they were. He's that way. He's attentive. He wants to know everything. You always hear that 'sponge' term. That's kind of where he's at in his career right now. You'd hope for Pat this is the right situation. You try to make it that way. Then he's got to go play. That's what it comes down to. But the situation should be one where he can achieve…He can't be in any better place than with the Kansas City Chiefs."

That made Kansas City a good landing place for Mahomes. He had a rookie season to adjust to the NFL game without the pressure of having to play. The biggest advantage might have been the presence of Reid, whom Mahomes' agent, Leigh Steinberg, called a "noted quarterback whisperer." "I've represented probably 120 quarterbacks over these 44 years and seen careers shortened by the quarterback development curve being rushed," Steinberg said. "Nothing could have been better for Pat than sitting and watching. Kansas City was perfect for him: stable ownership, smart front office, gifted coaching, a head coach who had developed a number of quarterbacks, a team that was already winning, and the opportunity to learn behind a wily, winning, talented veteran quarterback. We were thrilled that it was Kansas City. There are so many situations he could have gone into that were less than desirable. It was like a marriage made in heaven that it worked out the way it worked out."

McNabb, who was drafted by the Eagles in the first round in 1999, agreed. "Patrick Mahomes couldn't ask for a better coach to get drafted by," McNabb said. "Andy's not a guy who runs his offense like a dictator who won't change the offense because it's worked for him in the past. Andy knows what's best for his quarterback, and he'll coach to [Mahomes'] strengths and what the strengths are of the team. He adjusts every year depending on what he has to work with."

Reid's ability to identify and develop a young quarterback was part of the reason he was hired by Chiefs chairman Clark Hunt in 2013. Even before Mahomes had opened the 2018 season as the Chiefs' starter, Reid seemed to know how things would turn out. "Andy is a pretty even-keeled guy," Hunt said. "But watching him at practice during the [offseason], seeing him at training camp, talking to him, he's clearly excited about what this 2018 team can do. He knows he has a bunch of outstanding offensive players and he's working on plugging Patrick Mahomes into that, hoping we can take the offense to another level and go get that trophy that we've been trying to get since Super Bowl IV. I'd say it's a bounce in his step. I know that's a hard thing to imagine when you're talking about Andy. But truly he seems energized. I think the thought of getting to take a young quarterback, mold him. I think it's hard for him not to be excited. When you have a young quarterback, it's not like you're near the end of the journey. You're at the beginning, and it should only get better each year."

Hiring Veach as general manager in 2017 was another key step. Dorsey joined the Chiefs in 2013 shortly after Reid was hired as head coach. Dorsey greatly improved the quality of the Chiefs' roster with his personnel moves, which included the drafting of tight end Travis Kelce in the third round in 2013, wide receiver Tyreek Hill in the fifth round in 2016, Mahomes in the first round in 2017, and running back Kareem Hunt in the third round in 2017. The Chiefs made the playoffs in three of Dorsey's four seasons as their general manager, including winning the AFC West in 2016.

Months after team chairman Clark Hunt said the Chiefs were planning to extend his contract, Dorsey was abruptly fired in June 2017. "I just became concerned about our ability to continue the success that we've had the last four years—or better yet—to build on that success and have a championship team," Hunt said. "We have very high aspirations. We want to compete for a championship every year. We want to get to the Super Bowl and win it. I just felt that if we were going to do that in the next three or four years, we needed to make a change. I do not want to come back to one specific thing, as I want to stay away from the issues that were part of the decision, but I will say: that to have a championship team, your personnel department needs to be functioning at a very high level. The other 31 teams generally have very strong personnel departments, and if we are going to build a championship team, you have to have a department that is functioning at a very high level."

The Chiefs hired the 39-year-old Veach to replace Dorsey. Veach had worked in the Eagles' player personnel department with Reid and had come to the Chiefs with Reid in 2013 as one of Dorsey's top assistants. "The thing that stood out to me in the interview process was really his vision for the construction of the roster," Hunt said after hiring Veach. "A general manager has a big impact on the roster in any given year. Brett's vision is very much long term and building a championship roster over two or three years. I think he really brings that mind-set to the job. Andy and I had a chance to talk about all of the candidates as I went through the interview process, and there were a number of them that I think he would have worked well with. But obviously given his historical relationship with Brett, he was excited that the decision at the end of the day was to name Brett as the new general manager."

Veach had worked alongside Reid for years, and Reid approved of his promotion to general manager. But Veach has very much been his own man with his own ideas, and one reason he was hired was that he wasn't afraid to disagree with Reid on matters he felt strongly about. "It's not like we are working together for four years, and we agree on everything," Veach said. "A lot of times we disagree. The one thing about Coach—and if you know Coach—he likes to surround himself with people who work hard and challenge him. I don't think Coach would have had respect for me if I was saying, 'Yes, yes, yes,' for 10 years. I think my ability to go in there and challenge him in different areas raised his game. And I think that he always understood that when I came to him with an idea, with a solution to a problem, that it was well thought out and well researched."

Veach identified Mahomes as the perfect quarterback prospect to work with Reid and play for the Chiefs early in his college career—long before many teams considered him a top draft pick or even a potential pro. He was the driving force behind the Chiefs' decision to make the big leap in the 2017 first round and then draft Mahomes. "He was the best quarterback in the draft," Veach said before Mahomes had ever played a game for the Chiefs. "There was no doubt in my mind that was the right decision."

But Veach made several bold moves since taking over, and many of them moved the Chiefs forward. In his first offseason, he traded Smith and cornerback Marcus Peters. He also signed free-agent wide receiver Sammy Watkins. His major acquisitions in 2019 included the trade for defensive end Frank Clark and signing safety Tyrann Mathieu. The talented but moody Peters was a problem for the coaches and would have been expensive to re-sign when his contract expired. Moving Smith was necessary to make way for Mahomes. Clark and Mathieu played major roles in improving a Chiefs defense that was so bad in 2018 that it kept them from Super Bowl. Even the signing of Watkins, who has often taken a secondary role behind pass catchers Hill and Kelce, paid off with big performances in the AFC Championship Game and Super Bowl.

Veach has also shown a keen eye for undeveloped talent. When the Chiefs needed a kicker during the 2017 season, instead of signing a veteran, he pulled young, untested Harrison Butker off the practice squad of the Carolina Panthers in 2017. He has developed into one of the NFL's best kickers. In 2018 Veach traded with the Dallas

Cowboys for a little-known rookie cornerback. Ward became a regular starter the following year and a reliable player. "We are always going to build through the draft," Veach said. "And we are going to put an emphasis on retaining our young players and keeping them in Kansas City a long time. We will be selective in free agency, but again we have always been big on this: attacking every transactional period—the waiver wire cut-down days, the street free-agent signings, strengthening our practice squad throughout the year. I think there are ways to get a competitive advantage on teams. I think we have been very good at that. Going forward, it will be an aggressive approach to attack each one with the primary focus being on the draft."

The final piece to the championship puzzle was overhauling their defense in 2019. The Chiefs played solid defense in the earlier seasons under Reid, but things had changed in recent years and came to a head in the 2018 AFC Championship Game when they couldn't make a key stop against Brady and the Patriots.

Shortly afterward, the Chiefs began a defensive renovation on a grand scale. In fact, it's difficult to imagine the Chiefs being able to reasonably do more in one year. They fired defensive coordinator Bob Sutton and reassigned or let go all of the other defensive assistant coaches. They released, traded, or allowed to leave as free agents several longtime starters, including Eric Berry, Justin Houston, Ford, Allen Bailey, and Steven Nelson.

Berry, Houston, and Ford in particular served the Chiefs well. Berry, a safety, was one of the most popular Chiefs players ever. He was diagnosed with lymphoma in 2014, which caused him to miss most of that season. But he was determined to return in time for the 2015 season and, after forcing himself to continue his workout regimen through his chemotherapy treatments, he did indeed play for the Chiefs in their 2015 season-opener against the Texans.

Berry, the Chiefs' first-round draft pick in 2010, was selected to play in the Pro Bowl five times and as a first-team All-Pro three times. He made many iconic plays for the Chiefs. None were bigger than when he returned an interception for a score on a Falcons two-point attempt for the winning points in a 2016 game in his hometown of Atlanta.

Berry's problem—the rotten luck with the cancer aside—was that he couldn't stay in the lineup. He missed most of four of his nine seasons with the Chiefs. He tore his ACL, a season-ending injury, on one of the first plays in 2011 and tore his Achilles tendon, a season-ending injury, in his first game of 2017. The end for Berry in Kansas City was bitter. In what would be his final game for the Chiefs—the 2018 AFC Championship Game against the Patriots—Berry was burned twice by New England tight end Rob Gronkowski for big plays on third downs. One came on the go-ahead touchdown drive late in the fourth quarter, and the other came in overtime moments before the winning score.

Although it didn't end well for Berry in Kansas City, he would be difficult to replace. The Chiefs signed Mathieu as an attempt to do so. "No doubt it'll be huge shoes to fill," Mathieu said shortly after signing with the Chiefs. "Eric Berry was always a guy I admired. He gave me a ton of inspiration, especially all the adversity and things he'd dealt with. It would have been an honor to play with him, but ultimately I think anytime you can kind of steer your own ship and get guys to believe in you and get guys to buy into you the same way Eric did, I think that's my plan to really come in. Hopefully, the community will embrace me, and my teammates embrace me, and I can do what Eric did here."

Houston had one of the NFL's all-time great pass rush seasons for the Chiefs in 2014. With four sacks of San Diego Chargers quarterback Philip Rivers in the season's final game, Houston finished the season with 22, a half sack away from the league's single-season record. But like Berry, many of Houston's seasons with the Chiefs were interrupted by injuries. After that fantastic 2014 season, he never played a full, 16-game season for the Chiefs and hadn't come close to meeting the sack standard he set in 2014. His most productive season in Kansas City after 2014 occurred three years later when he had 9.5 sacks. "It's always hard to move on from players who have been here. I think it certainly makes it more difficult when change involves long-standing members of the community and the locker room, certainly [when] talking about Eric Berry and Justin Houston," Veach said. "What two guys better exemplify that? As everyone knows, these guys were outstanding players. All the accomplishments on the field will certainly never be forgotten. The way we felt about both of those individuals, and even though we knew what we had to do as the organization, it did not make it easy. It was something that was very tough to do. And usually the right decisions are the toughest decisions. We did that. Again, can't say enough great things about those two guys. Those two players will always have a special place in our hearts here and in the community."

Ford was the Chiefs' No. 1 draft pick in 2014, but he didn't become a productive player until 2016, when he led the team in sacks with 10. He had 13 sacks in 2018 in what would be his final season with the

Chiefs. He would become something of a villain among Kansas City fans for lining up offside late in the fourth quarter of what would be his final game with the Chiefs, the AFC Championship Game against the Patriots. His penalty nullified an interception that would have allowed the Chiefs to run out the clock and advance to the Super Bowl. New England instead went on to score the touchdown that moved the game into overtime.

The Chiefs considered Ford a one-dimensional player—a pass rusher but not a run defender—and felt he wouldn't fit into their new defensive system. They traded him to the 49ers for a 2020 second-round draft pick. The Chiefs eventually traded with the Seattle Seahawks for Clark, Ford's replacement. Clark went on to have a significant role in the Chiefs winning the Super Bowl for the first time in 50 years but wasn't with the team when Ford committed his penalty against the Patriots. He still weighed in on Ford and the penalty during the week of Super Bowl LIV as the Chiefs prepared to face Ford and the 49ers. "I don't know [anything] about him," Clark said. "I couldn't name a stat. I don't know the school he went to. I just know he had lined up offside, and anybody, who lined up offside at a time like that, I feel like that's a dumb penalty at the end of the day. I'm sure he feels the same way. Personally, I've lined up offside before but not in that type of [situation]."

The Chiefs hired Steve Spagnuolo, a longtime assistant for Reid earlier in their careers with the Eagles, as Sutton's replacement. He hired a new staff and installed a 4-3 base system, replacing the 3-4. They then signed safety Mathieu, traded for end Clark, drafted safety Juan Thornhill, and brought in several other defensive regulars. That's a lot of new for one year. "I've been through this first-year thing a number of times," Spagnuolo said during training camp in 2019. "Sometimes it's gone really good and sometimes it hasn't gone so good."

This one took a little bit of time but eventually turned out so well that the Chiefs would have one of the greatest seasons in the history and certainly their best in the previous 50 years.

2

HILL GOES DOWN, AND
WATKINS STEPS UP

"Obviously, whenever someone with Tyreek's ability goes out, you wonder what's going to happen. But the best thing about this team—and you've seen it the last few years now—is whenever someone gets their opportunity, they step up and play. And we really pick each other up. So, I was glad the guys stepped up, made plays; and that was running backs, receivers, tight ends, and whatever it was. I mean, that's just how we roll. Whoever is given the opportunity to make the play, they make it…We always have confidence going into any game, no matter who we're playing. We knew Jacksonville had a very good defense. They played us really well last year, so we really prepared ourselves to do what we could to have success on the field. It's always good when you look back at it now, and all that hard work that we've put in the last few weeks really paid off."

—Patrick Mahomes after the Chiefs beat the Jacksonville
Jaguars on the road in their season opener despite
losing Tyreek Hill to injury in the first quarter.

ANDY REID ONCE SAID THAT Sammy Watkins coming out of college at Clemson was the best wide receiving prospect he had seen for years. Certainly, there was a lot to like in the 6'2", 200-pound Watkins, including his 4.43 speed. Reid and the Kansas City Chiefs paid Watkins like they meant it when he went on the free-agent market before the 2018 season. They gave him a three-year contract worth $48 million. That sum was based more on his still considerable potential than what he had produced during his first four NFL seasons—three with the Buffalo Bills and one with the Los Angeles Rams.

The signing made sense even at the hefty price tag. The Chiefs wanted to provide as much help as possible to Patrick Mahomes, their new starting quarterback. Watkins still seemed like a good bet to become a great receiver. He was still only 24, still fast, and playing with a quarterback as talented as Mahomes couldn't hurt. Watkins didn't provide much in his first year with the Chiefs. He was little more than a decent third option to Travis Kelce and Tyreek Hill, and that was only when he was healthy. Watkins missed six games with injuries and had just two games with more than 100 receiving yards, including the playoffs.

So when the Chiefs imagined their offensive stars before their 2019 season-opening game against the Jacksonville Jaguars on a broiling hot afternoon in Florida, Watkins was far down the list. They never considered Watkins would catch two touchdown passes, covering 117 yards, in the first quarter and add another score in the fourth quarter. He finished with nine catches for 198 yards and the three touchdowns in the Chiefs' 40–26 win. "We've seen it all offseason," Mahomes said. "The way he's prepared his body, the way he's practiced, he really understands the offense on a different level than he did last year. Whenever he got his number called, he made plays. He was back to his Clemson days."

The Chiefs came out offensively against the Jaguars like it was 2018 again by scoring 40 points. They entered the season optimistic they could score again in big numbers. It's an optimism that was once shared by every other team on the NFL's top 10 single-season scoring list, but none of the others at the end of the next season had kept pace. "We expect to score every single time we're on the field," said Mahomes, who led the 2018 offense that scored 565 points, the third highest total in NFL history. "We plan to go out there, have positive gains, and get the ball in the end zone or let Butker kick it in."

Mahomes and the Chiefs had plenty of reasons to be optimistic, mainly because the signal caller—the reigning NFL MVP—and all the other significant parts were back. But unforeseen things happened the following season to all of the other teams on the top 10 scoring list. The other nine teams saw a drop in points the next season. Eight of the nine dropped at least 16 percent, and seven of the nine at least 20 percent. Only one of the nine teams, the 2000 St. Louis Rams, led the league in scoring again the following season. All, like the 2019 Chiefs, started the next season with big plans. The reality was almost always something else, and that's a trend the Chiefs were fighting. "What I've seen is they're trying to challenge themselves to do better," Reid said. "It's kind of interesting to watch. There's a certain drive there. Their willingness to learn new things, the excitement of going out there every day and playing together, there's a certain pride in that group. They challenge each other. And Patrick is right in there with them. He's leading the pack on that. I think that's an important quality to have. They're growing together. These are young guys. They challenge each other in a healthy way. They love each other. They hang out off the field, they vacation together. There's a unique camaraderie between them."

Between personal appearances and filming multiple commercials that would air locally and nationally, Mahomes had a busy offseason. But he found time for football. He led some teammates on an excursion to the Turks and Caicos Islands shortly before training camp. That vacation included Mahomes throwing passes on the beach to some receivers. "Pat did a lot in the offseason," general manager Brett Veach said. "He hit a lot of shows and award ceremonies. I think everyone, myself included, wondered after a world tour like that, 'What's the mind-set like?' Any question we had about that was erased when we got to the offseason program. You could see how focused and dialed in Pat was. Once it was time to go, it was time to go. Andy is locked in, too. It starts with those two. It's a coach-and-quarterback league, and we have the best of the best at both positions."

The Chiefs' offensive coaching staff returned intact. Some 65 percent of 2018's receptions were caught by players still on the team, including Kelce, Hill, and Watkins. The Chiefs returned just 42 percent of last season's rushing yards after they released Kareem Hunt late in the 2018 season, but they averaged 32 points in seven games with Damien Williams in place of Hunt as the featured back, including in the playoffs. "Everyone's motivated to get better, and that starts with Pat, especially," Chiefs right tackle Mitchell Schwartz said. "First year starting, second year in the league, 5,000 [yards], MVP, basically every award they've created for best athlete, and he's out there more critical on himself then anybody. That sets the tempo for the rest of the offense to try to get better."

The Chiefs added to their collection of offensive talent. They signed running back LeSean McCoy, who was 31 years old and coming off the least productive season (514 yards, 3.2 yards per carry) of his

10-year NFL career. But McCoy had big seasons playing for Reid early in his career with the Philadelphia Eagles and wouldn't have to carry a huge load with the Chiefs, who had Williams as the starter.

Two of the Chiefs' draft picks, second-round wide receiver Mecole Hardman and sixth-round running back Darwin Thompson, showed in training camp and the preseason that they could have impacts as rookies. Each took a short pass and outran defenders to the end zone for a touchdown in the preseason. "We're taking it up a level [from] years past," Kelce said. "You can just tell from the coaches' excitement, to their attention to detail, to how guys are reacting to their coaching, this team is going to be awesome. We're going to have a lot of fun on the offensive side of the ball."

Then there was Reid designing the offense and calling the plays. He seems to know how to get the best from Mahomes and the other skill players. Reid said he spent much of his offseason drawing up what he called "Pat plays" designed to take advantage of Mahomes' considerable skills. Mahomes said the Chiefs' playbook carried little resemblance to that of 2018. "When you have a quarterback with this kind of skillset, you have limitless options as a coach," Veach said. "Then we have so much speed on offense. When you have that many fast options, the more creative you can get. There's a lot of room for the mind to roam, and Andy takes advantage of that."

With regard to Watkins, Veach acknowledged after the Chiefs signed him that he had been trying to bring him to Kansas City for some time. He tried to acquire Watkins the year before when the Bills were offering him around the league. But the Chiefs were already without their first-round pick in 2018, having sent it to the Bills in the Mahomes trade. For that reason Veach didn't want to part with their second-round pick that year as well. So he offered a third-rounder to the Bills, who took a better offer from the Rams, and Watkins played the 2017 season in Los Angeles. But Veach didn't give up and won Watkins in a bidding war during free agency. "He was one of the best receivers coming out in a long time," Veach said, "love the guy. It's just hard to acquire these guys. When we're sitting there in free agency and you see a 24-year old elite playmaker, you don't get those opportunities a lot. What we have and where we're going, we may not get this chance again."

The Chiefs signed Watkins for games like the one he had against the Jaguars. His first touchdown of the game—from 68 yards out—was the most impressive. Watkins ran a short route and sat in a zone with three defenders nearby. Watkins made the catch at the Kansas City 39, made a move to get past cornerback Jalen Ramsey, and turned on that 4.43 speed to run by defenders to get to the end zone.

The Jaguars blew a coverage and left Watkins alone on a 49-yard touchdown catch later in the first quarter. With the Chiefs at the Jaguars' 3 in the fourth quarter, Ramsey tried to jam Watkins at the line. Watkins shoved Ramsey away, giving him an opening in the end zone. "From the first one on, you saw him break tackles and split seams," Reid said. "There was no indecision after catches. You're talking about one of the best receivers I've ever seen coming out of college. I mean, he was phenomenal. This is what you saw, what you saw today."

Watkins promised before the season on his Twitter account that 2019 would the best season of his career, saying he was "sacrificing everything'" to get that done. What did he mean by that? "You can easily come here and do the right things, but are we doing the right things at home as far as watching film, eating the right things, taking care of your body?" He said. "As a young guy you can just eat everything, hamburgers and everything. As I get older, I'm kind of like, man, my weight fluctuates up and down. I'm trying to really have a balanced meal plan and get the right rest and come here every day and put all my energy and my soul and my spirit into what I do."

For that one game, Watkins looked like he would keep his promise. But the big season didn't develop. He didn't score another touchdown during the regular season, finishing with just the three from Jacksonville. He didn't have another 100-yard game. His next-best showing was 64 yards in a Week Three game against the Baltimore Ravens. He finished third on his team in catches (52) and yards (673). "It's the ebbs and flows of the season, who gets the ball, and who doesn't get the ball," Watkins said late in the regular season. "That's not my focus. I can't worry about what's going on, who's getting the ball, who's not getting the ball. My job and my focus is to dominate whoever's in front of me. I've just got to go out there and play fast and enjoy and have fun and ultimately get the win. That's where my mind-set is now: just winning football games."

Watkins has been an enigma for his six NFL seasons. He was drafted fourth overall by the Bills in 2014, but he never produced to that level while in Buffalo. In three seasons he never had more than 65 catches. He surpassed 1,000 yards just once. He played in all 16 games just once because of injuries. The Bills sent him to the Rams after those three seasons with a year left on his contract because they had made the decision they would not try to re-sign him when it expired. His production—39 catches, 593 yards—wasn't what the Rams expected. Those numbers didn't improve much in his two seasons with the Chiefs. "Don't let the production fool you," Veach said when the Chiefs signed Watkins. "If you watch the tape, the guy is open all the time, literally open all the time…Now, he had some injuries and bounced around a couple different places, and sometimes it takes some time to develop a cohesive deal with the quarterback and the offense and the rhythm and the timing. From a skill standpoint, he was the best player on our board in free agency."

Watkins acknowledged then that coming into a situation where Kelce and Hill were already established was difficult. But Watkins entered the Chiefs' situation willingly. He could have signed with some team that was without a Hill and a Kelce, one where he would have been the No. 1 receiving option. That may have meant taking less money than he received from the Chiefs. "I've played this game a long time," Watkins said. "I just know how it works. If the coach wants me to get 1,000 yards, I'll get 1,000 yards. That's not the position I'm in. I'm old enough to realize there's a lot of great players on this team, a lot of guys that have been here before me. I can't sit here and be selfish and say, 'This is my team, and I want 1,000 yards.' This is Tyreek Hill's team. This is Kelce's team. Do I want the ball more? Of course. Any wide receiver in the league wants the ball more, but I can't get mad at anyone because I'm not getting the ball. I think it's the coach's job to put me in that position. I can't really worry or focus on any of that. I still have to go out there and play for my teammates and do it in a positive way. That's what mind space I'm in right now, for sure. I can go out there and do whatever lead receivers do, whatever the Julio Joneses, the Tyreek Hills, the Travis Kelces do. Anybody you can name that's great, I can do the same thing. But I think I help the team just by going out on the field with my presence and my energy and just how I play the game. That's enough for me."

Earlier in his career, particularly when he played in Buffalo, Watkins would complain publicly at times when he didn't get the ball. But he hasn't publicly displayed any unhappiness with the Chiefs. "I was young and I was kind of ego tripping," Watkins said. "Now I'm kind of older and I understand it's a team goal, and every week it's going to change. Next week Tyreek might have 180 yards, or Kelce might have 180 yards, and I might have 30. It's going to switch up with all these star athletes running around. I know I'm not going to get 50 targets. That's not realistic. I kind of went to the Rams [in 2017], and it was the same situation. That kind of helped my game with blocking and just staying engaged and giving that fuel to other guys out there making plays."

Watkins acknowledged a lack of effort at times. Based off the 40 time he ran coming out of college, Watkins should win sprints against many of the Chiefs' other receivers and at least make it a race against Hill and Hardman. But one day he wasn't competitive with the other receivers, prompting Mahomes to call him out for a lack of effort. "It was a good thing because the next day I came in first just about almost every rep," Watkins said. "[Mahomes] looked at me like, 'Yeah.' I was like, 'Yeah, I got it, bro. I'm on it.' He's the leader now. He kind of got on me a little bit, but that's what we need from a guy that leads this team."

Watkins may have disappointed most of the regular season, but he came up big in the playoffs. He had 114 yards in the AFC Championship Game against the Tennessee Titans and scored the clinching 60-yard touchdown midway through the fourth quarter that gave the Chiefs an insurmountable 18-point lead.

Then Watkins had 98 yards in the Super Bowl. His 38-yard catch in beating Richard Sherman was the biggest play on the go-ahead touchdown drive in the fourth quarter. Veach and the Chiefs are all too happy to accept mostly average results from Watkins in the regular season if he'll produce like that in the biggest of games. "You don't make moves to make the playoffs," Veach said after the AFC Championship Game. "We've been a playoff team for years since we got here. We were in the playoffs every year. You make moves like that to put you over the top. Without Sammy's performance today, who knows how this game would have turned out? I was happy for Sammy. He's around a lot of talent. So sometimes he can't show what he can do."

3

THE LEGION OF ZOOM

"I never take it for granted. Some of these throws he makes, you just say, 'All right' and buzz right through it like it happens every day. It kind of does happen. That's what makes him unique, and the fact that he's willing to continue to work on his game the way he does is also very important. In this league if you let off an inch, then you're going to fall. He stays right on top of that in everything that he does."

—Andy Reid on the play of Patrick Mahomes after the Week Two road victory against the Oakland Raiders.

THE KANSAS CITY CHIEFS ENTERED the offseason in 2019 with perhaps the fastest pair of starting wide receivers in the NFL in Tyreek Hill and Sammy Watkins. As their third wide receiver, they had Demarcus Robinson, who ran a 4.59 40 at the NFL scouting combine upon leaving college at the University of Florida. So he wasn't in the speed class of the others, but he could still scoot. They also had Travis Kelce, who is fast for a 260-pound tight end. That wasn't enough receiving speed to suit the Chiefs, who used their initial draft choice on Georgia's Mecole Hardman, who ran a 4.33 40 at the combine. The Chiefs receivers picked up the collective nickname of "The Legion of Zoom."

The Chiefs put all of this speed on display in the second quarter of their Week Two game against the Oakland Raiders. The Raiders were moving to Las Vegas for the 2020 season, so this was the Chiefs' final game at the Oakland Coliseum. The Chiefs trailed 10–0 entering the quarter and then scored 28 points, leaving the Raiders in the dirt of the Coliseum's baseball infield, which was grassless on this September afternoon because the baseball A's still had home games to play.

The Chiefs' touchdowns were all passes and came from 44, 42, 27, and 39 yards. The Chiefs had scoring drives of 95 and 94 yards on consecutive possessions. Patrick Mahomes threw for 278 yards in the second quarter alone. His final five pass attempts of the quarter were all completions and went for 42, 32, 43, 27, and 39 yards. Three were touchdowns. "It's the [biggest] fun rush I've had in my life, man," Kelce said. "And that's what you want every single week is to come out and to feel unstoppable. We did in that moment."

They left the Raiders more than a little shell-shocked after being so unable to cope with the Chiefs' speed. "A couple of those were just incredible throws and catches," Oakland coach Jon Gruden said. "You have to tip your hat to them. We didn't get enough pressure. We let Mahomes move around back there and cock his arm, and when he gets an opportunity to do that, he can drop them in there no matter where they are."

After suffering a sterno-clavicular injury against the Jacksonville Jaguars, following a hard tackle from cornerback Jalen Ramsey, Hill didn't play against the Raiders. The Chiefs also didn't get much from Watkins. But Hardman had the first touchdown of his NFL career, Robinson had 172 yards and two touchdowns, and Kelce had 107 yards and a score. "I don't think it was any point to prove that we can do it, I guess you would say, without Tyreek," Mahomes said. "It was just running the offense the way we run it. We're not going to change what we do. I mean, obviously we want Tyreek out there. He's [a] one-of-a-kind player, someone that's special on the field. But we're going to run our offense the way we run it, and guys are going to step up and make plays when their numbers are called. I think that's one thing about this offense. I just go through my reads, and whoever is open is open. I just try and give them the chance to make plays. I thought that they focused on trying to take away Sammy after his big game last week, and that gave other guys opportunities to make plays. That was how we rolled on offense. Every week it's someone else who makes plays, and if we can keep doing that, then hopefully we'll keep having success."

The receivers acquired their Zoom nickname in training camp when it became apparent how all of their speed would make the Chiefs difficult to defend. Veteran fullback Anthony Sherman arrived at camp that summer in Clint Bowyer's NASCAR racer—an outrageous prop but also one fitting for that season's Chiefs. After climbing out of the vehicle, Sherman claimed the car would be necessary to keep pace with an offense blessed with plenty of speed. "The only way I'm going to keep up with these young kids is to ride in this," Sherman said.

The Chiefs' receiving speed was jolting to safety Tyrann Mathieu, who joined the team in 2019. He said he had never seen an offense as fast as that of the Chiefs. "I had Bruce Arians in Arizona," Mathieu said of his former coach with the Cardinals. "He loved fast guys. But I've never quite played on a team or against a team [like this]…In my opinion this is probably the best 7-on-7 football team ever, just with all the talent they have on offense. There's a lot of guys you have to account for…They have a plethora of guys that can get it done. You add to it with a great quarterback, a guy that can put the ball anywhere on the field. He just always seems to find the open guy. Rarely does he throw interceptions. Anytime you can play with a quarterback that takes care of the ball, knows where the ball is supposed to be, it's always going to stress the defense."

The Chiefs had a big-play offense in 2018 but were anticipating even more during camp of 2019. Kelce was asked what all that speed would allow the Chiefs to do. "Anything we want," he said. "You name it. We've got 4.2, 4.3, maybe 4.1. I don't know what Tyreek runs now. Who knows? We've got guys that can absolutely fly all over the field. Speed kills in this game. If you've got it, you're in the advantage. We're taking it up a level [from] years past. You can just tell from the coaches' excitement, to their attention to detail, to how guys are reacting to their coaching. This team is going to be awesome. We're going to have a lot of fun on the offensive side of the ball."

The Chiefs finished the season second in the league in passes of 25 yards or more with 42. But they also scored 16 touchdowns on those plays—the most in the NFL and five more than any other team. Mahomes couldn't imagine a faster receiving group. "I can't, honestly," Mahomes said. "We've got guys that can roll, guys that really stretch the field. It really makes my job a lot easier. We're able to stretch the field vertically and horizontally. You can either take the deep pass and throw it like that or throw it out in the flat, and these guys can all take it 70 yards to the house. Defenses have to really pick and choose which matchups they want to take. We look at the matchups and trust that the receivers are going to win."

The game in Oakland was by far Robinson's most productive of the season. On many teams he would be a starter and perhaps a star. On the Chiefs, who drafted the fourth-round pick in 2016, he's often a role player who takes the scraps that more well-known receivers like Kelce, Hill, and Watkins don't get. "You have to be patient," Robinson said. "We've got a lot of great guys in the room, and they've been here longer than I have, and their number gets called more times than mine."

Up until the game in Oakland, Robinson had been known more for doing the little things such as throwing a block that sprung Watkins for his long touchdown catch the week before against the Jaguars. "He's a guy that kind of gets lost in the shuffle of things sometimes," Mahomes said. "He's a guy that's super-talented, makes a lot of big plays happen. It's everything from catching the ball on scrambles, catching touchdowns as the last read across the middle of the field, or making the blocks and doing whatever he can to help his teammates out."

The Raiders game was a peek of things to come from Hardman. His speed was a factor for the Chiefs all season. Counting a kick-off he returned for a touchdown, Hardman scored seven times as a rookie. All came from long distance. His scores were from 42, 83, 21, 30, 63, 48, and 104 yards. Most of those happened when he just ran away from defenders. He had two of the league's top 10 ball carrier speeds during the regular season, according to the NFL's Next Gen Stats. He was measured at 21.87 mph in scoring a 63-yard touchdown against the Tennessee Titans in Week 10 and 21.74 mph in scoring an 83-yard touchdown against the Baltimore Ravens in Week Three.

"I definitely had to step up," Hardman said after the Chiefs' 28–10 victory against the Raiders. "With [Hill] not on the field, he is a valuable asset. He is one of the best receivers in the league, so when you don't have that production on the field, you feel obligated to step in."

The Mahomes-Hardman football relationship got off to an unusual start. Hardman wasn't used to playing with such a strong-armed quarterback and occasionally didn't finish downfield routes or plays. He felt he was so far away that he wasn't going to get the ball. This frustrated Mahomes to the point that Robinson stepped in to give the rookie wide receiver some advice. "Just run through everything," Robinson said he told Hardman. "It's a different level of speed in the NFL than it was in college. We have the best quarterback in the NFL. He can get the ball downfield even when you're 60 yards downfield. So run through everything if you have a deep route and run full speed through all your routes."

Mahomes indicated by the end of offseason practice in June that Hardman had resolved the issue. "He's really starting to understand it," Mahomes said. "For him it's just knowing you're never dead; you always have a chance to catch the ball. I feel like that was something that he really picked up quick and started to excel at in the end."

Mahomes then had advice of his own for Hardman as it related to the upcoming training camp. "To make sure his legs were ready," Mahomes said. "That was the biggest thing. When you get to a football camp in the NFL, I mean it's full go every single play. There are no off reps. You are going every single rep…Every single rep is important. You can't take any rep off because you don't know if that is the rep that can get you to the Super Bowl in the end."

The Chiefs didn't always use their speed as effectively as they did against the Raiders, but it was something opponents always needed a plan for. "Not many teams you look at the roster, there's 4.2 something, three guys 4.3—there's just so many guys that are fast," New England Patriots safety Devin McCourty said in December before a Chiefs–Patriots game. "And you talk about getting vertical. You can't just stand over one guy and do it. They have multiple guys that can go vertical, and you have to play well at every position when you're in coverage because there's a threat of a guy going deep on every play. Right away, you think of the speed guys, but Kelce's another guy that can go deep. He's one of their better deep threats as well. So I think the toughest thing with the deep ball is the speed and the ability they have across the board, no matter who they put on the field."

One of Andy Reid's top priorities after joining the Chiefs in 2013 was to upgrade the team's speed. That was particularly true at wide receiver, where the Chiefs had been trying to get by mostly with plodding players. One of the first free agents the Chiefs signed after Reid's arrival was wide receiver Donnie Avery, who had 4.27 speed. But Avery was little more than fast. He lasted just two seasons with the Chiefs, catching 55 passes and scoring two touchdowns.

The Chiefs tried with others, most notably Jeremy Maclin, who had played for Reid with the Philadelphia Eagles. But Maclin had just one big season for the Chiefs before his career tailed off. The Chiefs finally got it right with a speed receiver in 2016, when they drafted Hill. He ran a 4.24 40 coming out of college but was available to them in the fifth round of that year's draft because he looked like trouble. He had pleaded guilty in Oklahoma in 2014 to punching and choking his pregnant girlfriend.

His arrival changed everything. He not only was fast, but he was also a versatile player. He could get off a bump at the line of scrimmage, run good routes, adjust to the ball well downfield, and win jump balls against taller defenders because of his leaping skills. Having Hill and other fast receivers in the lineup became even more important after the Chiefs drafted Mahomes in 2017 and promoted him to a starter the following season.

The Chiefs got confirmation Mahomes and Hill were going to be a nice pairing during the preseason in Mahomes' first season as a starter. Mahomes threw a pass late in the first half that travelled more than 70 yards. Hill ran past two defensive backs and used his excellent ability to track the deep pass to haul in the throw for a touchdown.

Hill didn't play against Oakland, but his speed was in play in the Super Bowl. He was measured at 20.45 mph on his 44-yard catch in the fourth quarter that started the Chiefs' rally from a 10-point deficit. That was the fastest speed of any play in the Super Bowl. In fact, seven of the nine fastest Super Bowl speeds were registered by the Chiefs despite the fact they played against another one of the NFL's speediest teams, the San Francisco 49ers.

The Chiefs' speed is put to good use by some imaginative play designs and calls. In the Super Bowl, Reid busted out a play he had first seen while watching a video of the 1948 Rose Bowl game between Michigan and USC. Reid came across the film of that game after his brother gave it to him. His brother's high school coach played in that game for USC. The Chiefs even called it on fourth down in the first quarter. It featured four players in the backfield, including Mahomes, doing spins before the snap, which went directly to running back Damien Williams. He gained four yards for a first down and set up the Chiefs' first touchdown. "We kept working on it every single week and kept executing it and doing it the right way, waiting for the perfect time to call it," Mahomes said. "When we were there, and Coach said it, I was like, 'It's time so let's do it.'"

The Chiefs have many times borrowed ideas for plays while watching video of college players in preparation for a draft. In the case of that long ago Rose Bowl, Reid said he had pulled more plays from that game and would use them in 2020. He was probably joking, but given his success for finding plays in unusual places and making them work in games, maybe he wasn't. "There's some good stuff in there," Reid said.

Reid's offensive coordinator is Eric Bieniemy. Former Chiefs assistant coach Brad Childress described Bieniemy as a "descending veteran" when they first crossed paths in 1999 with the Eagles. Childress was an assistant coach for Philadelphia, and Bieniemy was a reserve running back. Bieniemy still caught the eye of Childress, the Eagles' new head coach in Reid, and the rest of the coaching staff and eventually made the roster for his special teams skills. "He understood that was his value to our team as a special teams guy," Childress said.

Childress, who later gave Bieniemy his first NFL assistant job coaching Adrian Peterson and the running backs on the Minnesota Vikings, remembers his drive and enthusiasm as a player. Bieniemy got ready for practice an hour early. "I just have a picture of him, coming out on the practice field," Childress said. "We started right out with special teams, and he wanted to be able to go full tilt to start with. His level of detail when he prepared himself to play was incredible."

That same quality helped Bieniemy become an effective offensive coordinator years later for the Chiefs. He arrived with Reid in 2013 as the Chiefs' running backs coach and was promoted in 2018 after the Chiefs lost Matt Nagy, who moved on to become head coach of the Chicago Bears.

Reid calls the offensive plays while Bieniemy helps assemble the playbook and weekly gameplans and runs the offensive meetings. He's also the voice in Mahomes' ear through the headset on gamedays while relaying the play calls. Those aren't jobs Reid would trust to just anyone. "Quarterback is a detailed position," Reid said. "It's very easy to go, 'Ah, we can let that one slide.' That's not how he goes about it. He's going to make sure everything is covered. I trust him for that. I can't be there every second. He jumps in and just takes charge, and I have full confidence in him so I can go be the head coach, and he can run the offense. He does a heck of a job with it. When he brings it, he's bringing it, and it's every day. He doesn't let one thing slide."

Bieniemy wasn't the most skilled of players, but he lasted nine NFL seasons because of his mastery of the little things. Beyond his special teams work, he developed into a reliable third-down back because he figured out defenses, coverages, and blitzes. He now transfers that knowledge to others. "I take a lot of personal pride in making sure everything is dotted, T's are crossed, and everything is absolute," Bieniemy said.

Chiefs running back Spencer Ware gave Bieniemy credit for helping resurrect his career in 2015 when he joined the Chiefs after being released by the Seattle Seahawks. Ware went on to lead the Chiefs in rushing in 2016. "The biggest thing Coach Bieniemy brings to our offense is his intensity," Ware said. "If you take a look at his resume, and the players he's coached, and the way they play football each and every play...having an entire offense with that same mentality is pretty exciting."

Mahomes said Bieniemy's gameplan preparation is a big factor in his success. "He does not let me miss any detail of what the play is supposed to do, what the protection is supposed to be, and that helps me a ton because when we get to the game everything is a little bit easier," Mahomes said.

Bieniemy was legendary for how hard he got after Peterson during their days together with the Vikings. "He coached Adrian Peterson as hard or harder than anybody,'" said Childress, who was an assistant coach for Reid with the Chiefs for five seasons. "He was unmerciful. He was not about to let him be just a guy. Eric made sure he stepped with the right foot. He made sure he understood pass protection and how he fit into the passing scheme. For years he had just been a tailback, and they handed him the ball and told him to run. Eric taught him how to play the game. He would drill down and ask him after a play, 'What were you looking at on that run? What did the defensive tackle do? You can't tell me? Then you can't run that play if you can't tell me.' He would throw him out of drills for that.'"

Bieniemy interviewed for multiple NFL head coaching positions over the last two years but didn't get a job offer. "He'll be a good head coach one day," Peterson said. "It was good being coached by him because we were able to pick up a lot from him. I always knew he would be more than just a running backs coach."

Reid, who believed the Chiefs would lose Nagy at the end of the 2017 season, began grooming Bieniemy that season to eventually become the coordinator. Part of that grooming was getting Bieniemy to expand his scope from just the running backs, the running game, and the backs' involvement in the passing game. Bieniemy had some experience with that, though it didn't go particularly well. He was the offensive coordinator at the University of Colorado in 2011 and 2012, but the Buffaloes won a total of just four games. "The thing I started focusing on is just seeing the bigger picture, understanding what the quarterbacks are looking at, how they're seeing it, what their progression is, just basically taking the big picture of everything," Bieniemy said. "Just basically taking notes from a different perspective has helped. It helped a huge amount."

4

BATTLE OF THE MVPS

"It's actually a pretty cool story. Me and Coach Reid and pretty much all the offensive coaches and quarterbacks, we go through our four-minute situations every week, and I've done it for three years now and we finally call a play we had already prepared for the night before. It just shows that every detail matters. We talked about that play the night before, and you think people would let that go after not calling it for a couple years now, but we had it prepared, we called it, and we succeeded when we got the opportunity to run it."

—Patrick Mahomes on a late-game, third-down
screen pass to Darrel Williams that allowed the
Kansas City Chiefs to run out the clock in Week Three.

LAMAR JACKSON OF THE BALTIMORE RAVENS in 2019 was to the NFL what Patrick Mahomes was the season before. He was the hot, young quarterback who could do no wrong in his first full season as a starter. He also would succeed Mahomes as the league's Most Valuable Player.

Mahomes showed his typical grace toward Jackson late in the season when it became obvious Jackson and not Mahomes was headed toward the MVP award. "Every single year it seems like someone is coming out and putting their stamp on the game and how you can go about having success here," Mahomes said. "Lamar is playing at an extremely high level right now not only with what he is able to do with his legs but the way he's able to get in the pocket and hit these seam throws and hit these shots down the field. You can understand with the more and more experience he's gotten, he's really understanding what defenses are trying to do to him. I think with him he's just playing at a great level right now."

Mahomes would, of course, get the bigger prize when the Chiefs won Super Bowl LIV. He also has the better of Jackson in their two regular-season, head-to-head meetings. The Chiefs in Week Three needed the best of Mahomes in their home opener against the 2–0 Ravens. The Chiefs played without Tyreek Hill, running back Damien Williams, and left tackle Eric Fisher, all of whom were sidelined because of injuries.

The Chiefs needed Mahomes to be better than Jackson, and he delivered by throwing for 374 yards and three touchdowns in a 33–28 victory that ran Kansas City's record to 3–0. Mahomes and the Chiefs also beat Jackson and the Ravens in a 2018 game, winning 27–24 in overtime. Mahomes' burgeoning reputation for being able to make unconventional plays that few other quarterbacks could make received a boost from a couple of interesting plays that led to that Chiefs' victory in 2019. A week after throwing for 443 yards in a win against the Oakland Raiders, Mahomes fell short of his second straight 400-plus-yard game this time. But he had his 13th game with at least 300 yards, giving him the NFL record for the most by a quarterback in his first 20 career starts.

Missing so many important pieces, the Chiefs relied on Mahomes more than usual. Mahomes attempted a pass on 25-of-34 first-half plays. He completed 20 and had two touchdowns, including an 83 yarder to Mecole Hardman that was the second longest scoring throw of Mahomes' career. Mahomes became the only player in the last 40 seasons with 250 passing yards and two touchdowns in the first half of three straight games. Mahomes and the Chiefs continued to roll despite all of their injuries. "It's the preparation Coach Reid puts us through during training camp," Mahomes said. "We get everyone in. Everyone gets reps with the [starters]. I think guys kind of build that confidence then to know that they can play whenever they get their name called."

Hardman's touchdown was another example of his blazing speed. He reached 21.7 mph on the play, according to the NFL's Next Gen Stats, but he said that was nowhere near his top speed. "I was about 80 percent, 85," Hardman said.

Perhaps that's some exaggeration on the part of Hardman. Perhaps not. Either way, the rookie wide receiver was doing a nice job of filling in for Hill by scoring his second long touchdown in two weeks. He was playing so well that the Chiefs would have to find playing time for him when Hill returned later in the season. In the meantime the Chiefs were working him into their offense with plays that allowed him to use his speed. Hardman got the ball on an end-around against the Ravens, and Mahomes tried unsuccessfully to throw him a pass on a bubble screen. But the deep ball is Hardman's calling card. The Ravens blew a coverage on his long touchdown and they had no chance to recover against a receiver with his kind of speed. He caught a 42-yard touchdown on a post pattern the previous week against the Raiders and had a 72-yard touchdown against Oakland called back because of a penalty.

Mahomes missed Hardman on a deep route earlier in the Ravens game, costing the Chiefs a big play. "I told him to just keep running, keep doing what he was doing, keep playing fast," Mahomes said. Hardman listened, and the two were rewarded with the long touchdown pass later in the game. "Once the ball gets in his hands, it's like the Tyreek effect," Mahomes said. "It's just about over."

Ravens safety Earl Thomas said during the week the Ravens would shut down Kansas City's flow of big plays. With Hill out of the game, it sounded like a plausible scenario. But the Chiefs had six plays of at least 20 yards and five of at least 25. "We're going to play our offense and do our offense the way we do it," Mahomes said. "We're going to have opportunities to beat people deep and we're going to execute on those. You can say it during the week, but we're still going to do what we do every single week."

Mahomes is 24, and Jackson is 23. Their rivalry looks to just be starting. They haven't faced off in the playoffs, but that matchup figures to be coming—perhaps multiple times. "That's a great quarterback," Jackson said. "I hate playing against him if you want to be honest and I'm not even on defense. He can throw the ball anywhere on the field, he can make every throw. He's what you want in your quarterback. That's a guy I love to compete against. He's going to give me a run for my money, and that's what I like about playing against him. I'm 0–2 against him right now. I've got to beat him soon, very soon."

Mahomes threw for 377 yards against the Ravens in his first matchup against Jackson in 2018, and the Chiefs needed every one of those yards to claim the victory in overtime. Two plays from the game stood out, and each added to the legend of Mahomes. The quarterback's use of the no-look pass started innocently enough. He fooled around with it in college and eventually worked his way up to a friendly practice competition with one of Texas Tech's other quarterbacks. Mahomes learned he was good at looking one way to steer a defender in the wrong direction and then getting the ball to a receiver in another part of the field. Suddenly, the no-look pass became something more than a practice prop for Mahomes. "I realized it was actually a tool I can use in games," he said.

He used it against the Ravens in 2018 late in the second quarter when he looked to middle of the field but threw to Demarcus Robinson on the left side for a 17-yard gain. The pass turned out to be a key play. It moved the Chiefs to midfield and allowed them to kick a field goal as the first half ended. Mahomes wasn't showing off on the play. The no-look component was necessary. It got Baltimore safety Chuck Clark to pause just long enough for Robinson to get open. "I was looking and I saw [Robinson] about to come open and I needed to move the safety over to the right," Mahomes said. "I just kind of trusted [Robinson] was going to be there and I put it out there, and he made a great play on it."

It wasn't the first no-look pass that Mahomes threw for the Chiefs, but it was the most effective. It wouldn't be the last. Mahomes tried the trick in the 2019 season opener but missed an open Travis Kelce, costing the Chiefs a touchdown. Still, none of his attempts have wound up in the hands of a defender. "I haven't thrown an interception yet," Mahomes said. "Hopefully, I won't. I tried to throw one earlier in the season and I think one of the receivers—it might have been Tyreek— stopped running because he was thinking I was going throw it back to the right. You just have to have that chemistry and know that he's going to keep running his route the same way."

Head coach Andy Reid, offensive coordinator Eric Bieniemy, and quarterback coach Mike Kafka have given Mahomes plenty of free reign with respect to his creativity in making plays. Mahomes hasn't abused the privilege. He has 76 touchdown passes with 18 interceptions for the Chiefs in the regular season. In the postseason his ratio is even better: 13 touchdowns and two interceptions.

That's proof he's making the right decisions. Mahomes has completed many a pass in an unorthodox style—whether that's no-look, across his body while moving to his left, or even left-handed. "They never encourage that," Mahomes said of Reid and his staff. "As long as you complete it and you get the first down, they're fine with it. At the same time, you have to know when not to do that. You never want to throw across your body as a quarterback, especially in this league, but it kind of happened naturally."

Mahomes didn't throw a ton of interceptions in college at Texas Tech: 29 in 1,349 pass attempts or on about 2.1 percent of his throws. But he was prone to try to make a play down the field when one wasn't necessarily available rather than always operate within the offensive system and be content with a shorter gain.

The Chiefs set about changing that part of Mahomes' game from the time he arrived. The first thing they did was have him observe Alex Smith, who protects the ball as well as any quarterback but isn't a playmaker in Mahomes' category. Smith threw an interception on just 1.4 percent of his throws in his five seasons with the Chiefs. "What he learned from Alex was having respect for the football," former Chiefs assistant coach Brad Childress said. "I've been around quarterbacks who have no regard for the football. If it became between you and the football, you can have the football. So Pat gets that part: how turnovers can kill you."

When Mahomes was a rookie in 2017, the Chiefs hired Kafka expressly to tutor him. Kafka once played for Reid with the Philadelphia Eagles and has since been promoted to quarterbacks coach. "Mike Kafka has lived with this kid now for two years," Reid said during Mahomes' first season as a starter. "Mike played in the offense, so he knows the rules and regulations you kind of have to go by but also the freedom you get to be yourself, to put your own mark on it. Then the kid is wired that way. He wants to do well and be the best. So you can coach him, and he will take his coaching and he'll work with you on it. It's a tribute to him. He's a special kid that way."

Reid routinely uses a trust test with his quarterbacks, asking them after certain plays during practice or games what he saw from the defensive coverage. Reid said Mahomes almost always breaks down the coverage exactly the way it unfolded. "Not every quarterback can spit that out to you," Reid said. "The thing about Pat is he's blessed with this great vision. He sees everything out there."

Because Mahomes is often aware of everything the defense is doing from the start of a play to the finish, Reid is comfortable in not placing many restrictions on him in terms of the types of throws he can make. As Reid put it, "You let him put his personality on it."

Childress said Mahomes as a rookie in practice made several no-look passes, gazing out into the flat while throwing a slant toward the middle of the field. "I coached Favre for two years, and he's the only other guy I've seen that was confident enough to be able to do that: to look one way and throw the other," Childress said. "[Mahomes] would do that in practice, and Andy, of course, would keep a straight face. He didn't encourage it at all, but you've got to let him be himself. He's got supreme confidence in his ability. You don't want somebody who doesn't. You wouldn't want somebody who doubts himself or questions himself."

Mahomes had some interception-filled practice sessions early in training camp during his first season as the starting quarterback. Reid described a lot of the interceptions as the result of Mahomes testing the limits of what he could get away with on certain plays and against certain coverages. He's thrown just 20 in regular season and playoff games, and few could be described as reckless. "Most guys are told not to do that," said fullback Anthony Sherman, referring to Mahomes' unconventional throws. "He goes out there and executes it and it's like, 'okay, I guess you can do that.' Coach Reid gives him the ability that if he thinks he can get it there, throw it and get it there. He knows he's going to have to get the ball into some tight windows, but he trusts his arm enough. I think at this point we should trust him and know he won't put us in a bad situation. He'll just find a way to get the ball to an open receiver."

It appears Mahomes will keep chucking, and the Chiefs will keep reaping the benefits. "It's all situational," Mahomes said. "Sometimes you can extend plays and give your receivers chances to make plays and sometimes you need to stay in the pocket and just take what's there. I'm not fast. I know my strength is not running the ball. I know I have a lot of playmakers whose strength is catching the ball and making people miss. I know if I keep my eyes downfield, I can get it to them."

Reid has seen a lot of passes during his long career, but even he marveled at Mahomes' accuracy on the no-look pass. "He's comfortable doing it," Reid said. "This is the NFL, and he's doing it. It's one thing to do it in practice, and then you start throwing it in a game—and a game against the No. 1 defense in the National Football League—that's a little different. You have to have tremendous confidence in what you're doing there. He's got a knack for that. He did a nice job with it. He actually froze [Clark] when you really look at it and what effect it had on the defense. There was a guy right underneath the route. I would have liked to interview that guy right at that point. That's a tough bind. How do you go explain that to your coach when he's looking over here, but he threw it over here? They're going to think you're crazy, right? But it worked."

Like some of the other unconventional throws Mahomes occasionally makes, the no-look pass can be a dangerous maneuver. Reid said he isn't going to stop Mahomes from doing it because the Chiefs would lose a lot of big plays if he did. "He's able to decipher the defense and kind of know where his guys are," Reid said. "You've got to put in the speed of the player and all those things. He's able to get that all spit and calculated out in his brain. He's got a knack for it. You heard this about Ted Williams, the baseball player, that he could read the stitches on the baseball. Certain guys have vision. They can see. [Mahomes] does have real good vision. I haven't seen a lot of guys do that. I was around Favre, who did some amazing things that way and Donovan [McNabb] and those guys but not quite like that."

Few if any quarterbacks could make the fourth-and-9 throw that Mahomes did later in the 2018 game against Jackson and the Ravens. With less than two minutes remaining and the Chiefs down by seven points, they needed to make a play to keep their hopes alive. The Ravens brought pressure up the middle and forced Mahomes to run to his right. While still on the move toward the sideline, he threw back across his body downfield to Hill, who made the catch for 48 yards and a first down. The Chiefs would go on to score the tying touchdown and eventually win in overtime. It was only another in a long line of big plays from Mahomes against Jackson and the Ravens.

Even without Hill's presence in 2019, Mahomes continued to flourish against the Ravens in his second meeting against them. Though Hill, his usual big-play receiver, was in the lineup for just part of the first quarter in the opener, Mahomes was averaging 398 yards per game along with 10 touchdowns and no interceptions. The Ravens game was the third straight with a different leading receiver. Travis Kelce had seven catches while Hardman had 97 yards, following big games from Sammy Watkins in the opener and Robinson in Week Two.

The Chiefs have more skilled receivers than most teams, but Mahomes had also mastered the art of keeping them all happy by knowing how to spread the ball around. "You want to utilize everyone's talent that we have out there," Mahomes said. "We try to get it in everyone's hands and let them make plays. It just makes the defense have to cover every single part of the field. It speaks to the weapons that we have as an offense. They can't stop everybody. So for me it's just about getting it to the guy that has the man-to-man coverage or has the open area."

As long as they're getting big plays and scoring points, the Chiefs don't care which of their players get the ball or how many times it happens. But they were aware the offense works better in the long run if Mahomes spreads the ball around to as many of the Chiefs' receiving threats as possible. Through three games the Chiefs had 101 points, and Mahomes' 10 touchdown passes had gone to five different receivers. "Everything is predicated on matchups," Bieniemy said. "Our goal each and every week is to make sure we're getting everyone involved. But sometimes the flow of the game may take you in a different direction. If everybody is having success in one particular game, we're obviously doing something right. That gives us a big chance to be successful."

To this point in the season, opponents were having trouble containing everything the Chiefs had going despite Hill's absence. This would continue for weeks even after Hill returned to the lineup. The Chiefs had a different receiver lead them in yards in each of their first six games of the season, and that list contained not only the bigger names like Watkins, Kelce, and Hill, but also the new or lesser-known receivers like Robinson, Hardman, and Byron Pringle.

Pringle had 103 receiving yards and a 27-yard touchdown in Week Five against the Indianapolis Colts. Mahomes had to scramble out of trouble on the touchdown, and it looked for a moment like the quarterback wouldn't be able to get him the ball. Something told Pringle to stay alert. That something was his quarterback. "One thing about Mahomes: you just stay alive and keep moving because he will find you anywhere on the field even if he is in the stands," Pringle said.

Pringle became the Chiefs' fourth 100-plus-yard receiver in their first five games. That's something the Chiefs had never done before, and it spoke loudly about their depth at wide receiver that one of those four receivers wasn't Hill. It also spoke to Mahomes' big-play ability. "Pat gives everybody a chance to be explosive," Robinson said. "Every week can be a big week for any of us guys."

Such receiving depth wasn't anything new for the Chiefs. Chris Conley was the Chiefs' third wide receiver in 2018, but he signed with the Jacksonville Jaguars in free agency before the 2019 season. He wound up catching 47 passes and scoring five touchdowns for the Jaguars.

The Chiefs merely moved Robinson into Conley's spot, drafted Hardman, and their offense again was productive. Any of the receivers can end up that week's star. "There's no telling," Mahomes said. "There will be games where teams will come in and try to take away one or two guys. That's the good thing about this team is that no one cares about who's getting the shine, I guess you would say. We'll spread the ball around to whoever's open. There are always plays Coach Reid draws up every single week. I always say they always work. He literally gets up on the board and starts drawing plays. The possibilities, like I said, are endless. You have to go at every single team a different way. Every single team plays different coverages."

Watkins figured to be the one player who benefitted most from Hill's absence. But he had been mostly quiet in the two games since his big game in Jacksonville. "When he's got that ball in his hands, he's an explosive runner," Reid said. "It's like having a running back when he's got that ball, big, strong, physical guy. I've got to make sure to do a better job of making sure I get it to him, keep him involved."

For his part Watkins kept his peace, as he had done since joining the Chiefs. "I've been in these situations before where there's been the outside noise: 'Oh, he's not getting his catches,'" Watkins said. "At the end of the day, we're winning the games. I'm going to continue to work hard and let everything play out. Even myself, I have to do the same thing. Being in Buffalo, being the guy demanding the ball, wanting targets, I've learned it's not all about me. It's about winning as a team. That's what it's about. I've grown to that. At first I had a bad time with that, not getting the ball. I'd be out there in the media probably saying something crazy three or four years ago. I'm not doing that now."

No matter the player getting the ball, the Chiefs were finding a way to make it work. "That says a lot about Coach Reid and what this organization has been able to bring together," Kelce said after the Ravens game. "Sammy Watkins showed everybody some stuff and opened some eyes to show he's the real deal. It's based off what the defense is showing. Pat has great awareness, great feel in the pocket and, sure enough, he was throwing the ball all over the field. It was a day to exploit matchups, and today I guess I was open more than usual."

5

LESS IS MORE

"You fight through adversity. It wasn't just the offense, wasn't just the defense, it wasn't just special teams. As a whole we just found ways to pick each other up whenever the other was struggling. In this league it's not always going to be pretty, it's not always going to be 50 points and three-touchdown wins. You're going to have to find a way to win these games against great teams. So for us we know that this win—not playing our best football and still finding a way to win—is going to help us tremendously as we get to the end of the season."

—Patrick Mahomes after the fourth-quarter comeback to beat the Detroit Lions in Week Four.

For those who didn't see the Kansas City Chiefs' Week Four road contest against the Detroit Lions, it would be easy to conclude Patrick Mahomes didn't have much of an impact on his team's 34–30 win. He failed to throw a touchdown pass for only the fourth time in his career. His streak of regular-season games with at least two scoring passes was over at 14—one shy of Peyton Manning's NFL record.

Those who played in the game know the Chiefs' victory had the Mahomes imprint as big as ever—even if not statistically. "On the final drive, he made every play we needed him to," Chiefs tackle Mitchell

Schwartz said after Mahomes took the Chiefs on a 79-yard winning drive. "He won't play a game where he's not the most important player on the field. It doesn't matter what the stats show."

Mahomes engineered that go-ahead touchdown with 20 seconds left. "As a leader on this team, [Mahomes] kept us collected and kept us with one goal in mind, and that's to get the ball in the end zone no matter how long it takes us to get it there," Travis Kelce said. "Whether it takes us one play or 16 plays, 20 plays, it doesn't matter. We're going north and we're getting the ball in that end zone. I think Pat does an unbelievable job of rallying the troops when we need it the most."

The Chiefs needed that more from Mahomes in Detroit than they had at any point so far in the young season. The Lions went on to win just three games all season but were pesky to the eventual Super Bowl champions on this afternoon. The Lions played a lot of man coverage, and the Chiefs' receivers had trouble most of the game in shaking loose. The Chiefs trailed 30–27 after the Lions' go-ahead touchdown with two-and-a-half minutes left in the game. They didn't have much reason to feel good about their chances at a winning touchdown. The Chiefs hadn't moved the ball consistently all game. One of their touchdowns, a 100-yard fumble return by cornerback Bashaud Breeland, came on defense.

But they had Mahomes, and on this day, like many others, that was enough. "He never gave up, first of all," Andy Reid said. "Very easily a young guy can get in the tank if the things aren't going right. Whether it's his problem or somebody else's problem, you start pointing the finger or you point the finger at yourself when you go in the tank. He didn't do that at all. He just kept it going. He said, 'We're going to win the game. We just have to kind of get rid of some of this garbage here.' They played man coverage, and you're going to have some big [plays] and then you're going to have some ones that don't look so good, but we know that. We knew that coming in. We were still able to score some points, which was important, and come out with a win."

To further illustrate what an usual Sunday it was for the Chiefs, seldom-used running back Darrel Williams scored two touchdowns, including the game-winner. Two others, who played mostly on special teams, tight end Deon Yelder and wide receiver Byron Pringle, contributed big plays.

But most of all, the star was Mahomes. He rushed for 54 yards, which was almost enough to make him the team's rushing leader for the game. But his rushing would be an important part of the Chiefs' success as the season went on. He led the team in rushing in a Week 11 win against the Los Angeles Chargers and in both of their playoff games. In the Super Bowl, Mahomes rushed for just 29 yards. But his 12-yard run was a key play on the Chiefs' first touchdown, which was scored by Mahomes on a one-yard run.

Mahomes was 6-of-9 for 55 yards on the final drive in Detroit, but his most important play was his scramble for 15 yards on fourth down to keep the winning drive alive. It was enough to frustrate the Lions, who were prepared for a barrage of Mahomes passes but not necessarily runs. "He's definitely a crafty guy," Lions defensive end Trey Flowers said. "Obviously, he's aware in the pocket. He's a guy that's able to move around. Obviously, guys up front have to understand how he's able to make some plays with his legs. We just had to keep him in the pocket [and] we missed a few opportunities."

Mahomes just shrugged afterward about his ability to pull out the win despite a less-than-ideal offensive performance. "Just finding whatever way to win the football game," he said, "that's how you roll in this league. It's not always about the touchdowns and the yards. It's about finding a way to win. If that was running for the first down, if that was handing the ball off...I'm going to do that. If you want to be great as a team, as a player, it's how you win the game. So for me I'm just going to go out there every single week and do whatever it takes to win. I think the whole message that I had the whole second half to my teammates and in the huddle was: 'be who we are.' It's not about someone having to do something spectacular. It's not about someone having to do and be more than themselves. It's about believing in each other and just being who we are and then letting everything fall in line."

Mahomes' 2019 season was a different experience for both himself and the Chiefs than the one before it. In 2018 Mahomes burst onto the scene with as big a debut starting season as anyone ever had. He became only the second player to throw 50 touchdown passes while also exceeding 5,000 yards. The first was Manning. Mahomes was selected as the NFL's MVP in his first try.

He got off to a great start in 2019 with 10 touchdown passes in the first three games. Then came the game in Detroit. It started a streak of six games, in which he would throw just five touchdown passes, though he would miss two of those games because of a knee injury. He finished the season with 26 touchdown passes and just over 4,000 yards. The stats were still good enough to be the second best quarterback season in Chiefs' history. But they were so far from his 2018 pace that at times it looked like he had an average season for an

NFL passer or at least had taken a step backward as a quarterback. He relinquished the NFL's MVP award to a fellow young quarterback, Lamar Jackson of the Baltimore Ravens.

As a team the Chiefs scored 451 points—114 fewer than in 2018, when they were No. 1 in the NFL. On average they scored about a touchdown less per game. "It really put in perspective how hard it is to go out there week by week and put up numbers and get wins," Mahomes said. "It's a struggle in this league. Teams are coming with their best effort, playing us really hard. I realized this year that it's better just to find ways to win rather than try to put up all these numbers."

The Chiefs would say he was a better player in 2019 despite what the statistics showed. "He's learning how to win when things aren't perfect," offensive coordinator Eric Bieniemy said. "Now he's making plays with his feet in the pocket. He's making a call at the line of scrimmage and giving us an opportunity to pick up pressure from a late-rotating safety. Don't get me wrong: you always want to see those games where we can have 400, 500 yards passing and a lot of points. But you have to know how to win when things aren't perfect."

Things weren't perfect for Mahomes in 2019. After spraining his left ankle in the season-opening win against the Jacksonville Jaguars, Mahomes was listed on the Chiefs injury report every day until the last week of the regular season. At one point late in the season, Mahomes said he felt better physically at that time than he had since the week leading up to the Jaguars' game. Mahomes had his right kneecap shift out of place during a Week Seven game against the Denver Broncos, causing him to miss the two games. He bruised his passing hand trying to break his fall during a Week 14 win against the New England Patriots, and it took some time before that injury resolved itself.

The Chiefs also went through a rash of injuries early in the season that cost Tyreek Hill four games and left tackle Eric Fisher eight. The Chiefs were forced to start five different offensive line combinations throughout the season because of injuries. A running game is a quarterback's best friend, but Mahomes was forced to do without one many times during the season. The Chiefs rushed for 98 yards per game in 2019—18 per game fewer than in 2018.

"He set the bar so high for himself last year," said former Chiefs quarterback Rich Gannon, who announced some of the team's games as a TV analyst for CBS. "But he still had a great season. If you take Lamar Jackson out of the mix and if he doesn't miss those two-and-a-half weeks, I think he's going to finish in the top three of the MVP voting anyway. If he didn't get hurt, this would have been a lot closer race. He didn't have as many touchdowns as he had the last year. He didn't have 50 touchdowns, but the thing that's amazing to me is that he has [five] interceptions. That's just as impressive when you look at the number of times he's thrown the ball, and look at the number of weeks they were banged up at running back, or when they weren't running the football well, and look at the number of weeks they didn't have Eric Fisher. You start looking at all that and you see a lot to like when you study this guy."

Whether Mahomes had to redeem himself for the regular season or not, his playoffs were spectacular. He threw eight touchdown passes and for more than 600 yards in the two AFC playoff games. He threw two interceptions in the Super Bowl but saved his best for the final nine minutes. With the Chiefs down by 10 points, he threw two touchdown passes to lead them back to a victory.

He was named Super Bowl MVP and for that alone will have an elevated place in team history. But there's so much more to the story. "Anytime you've got a quarterback that doesn't necessarily look at the scoreboard, it always feels like he's in it even when he may not be having his best day," Tyrann Mathieu said. "His demeanor doesn't change whether we're up by 30 or down by 10 points. It feels good to have a quarterback like that. It goes through the locker room. It goes through the team. We always feel like we've got a shot."

Mahomes had help that day against the Lions, and much of it came from unexpected places. The Chiefs' final two touchdowns against the Lions were scored on one-yard runs by Darrel Williams, a running back who wasn't even a starter in college at LSU. Darrel Williams' winning touchdown came with 20 seconds left in the game. Even in 2019 there were times when Darrel Williams was no better for the Chiefs than fourth in line for playing time at his position. But he delivered when the Chiefs needed him. In the previous week's game against the Ravens, his third-down conversion on a screen pass allowed the Chiefs to run out the clock rather than give the ball back one final time to Jackson. Then came his two fourth-quarter touchdowns against the Lions. "It's just who Darrel Williams is," Bieniemy said. "He was that way at LSU. If you pay attention and watch him, [it isn't] by chance that things happen for him on gameday. The kid prepares himself. He understands what it takes to win. Whatever role you want him to step into, that's the role he's going to assume, and that's the role he will play. The kid has no fear of what he does. There's no stage too big for him."

Darrel Williams hadn't been asked to deliver in big moments much during his career. At LSU he was teammates with Leonard Fournette and Derrius Guice, so he started just six games in four years. Darrel Williams said he never seriously considered transferring to find more playing time because he thought being around top backs daily would make him a better player. "My biggest thing is being able to compete," he said. "I saw the things they did every day and tried to make those things part of my game. I knew I had to work hard for playing time."

He signed as an undrafted rookie in 2018 with the Chiefs, who at the time had the NFL's leading rusher from the season before, Kareem Hunt. He could have picked a team with an easier path to playing time. "That was the same thing as my college decision," Darrel Williams said. "I wanted to be able to compete with the top back in the NFL."

Darrel Williams has an obvious belief in his ability. "If you talk to Darrel, Darrel will tell you he can do it all," Bieniemy said. "I've been told that quite a few times by Darrel."

The Chiefs released Hunt late in the 2018 season, but at one stage of training camp in 2019, Darrel Williams was fourth on the depth chart at running back behind Damien Williams, Carlos Hyde, and rookie Darwin Thompson. Darrel Williams eventually passed Thompson, and Hyde was traded to the Houston Texans, but the Chiefs then put another obstacle for playing time in his way by signing veteran LeSean McCoy shortly before the start of the season. Darrel Williams just shrugged that move off, too. "It was just another guy I had to compete with," Darrel Williams said. "It's just something that made me work harder."

Between Damien Williams' injury and McCoy's unreliability with ball security—his two fumbles in upcoming games were costly for the Chiefs—they turned to Darrel Williams first against Baltimore and then Detroit. "That was a nice cookie that he gave himself for saying, 'Listen: I busted my tail, I dropped my weight down, increased my body mass muscle-wise, and this is the result,'" Reid said. "That helps you keep pushing through all of that. He's naturally a big guy. I thought he played physical. I thought he did well in the pass game. Some of his blitz pickups [were] top-notch."

The Chiefs weren't afraid to play Darrel Williams on the third-and-9 play against the Ravens when he took the screen pass 16 yards to effectively end the game. "Coach trusted in me, believed in me," Darrel Williams said, sounding not surprised but grateful. "Just being in that position meant a lot to me with the game being on the line."

In Detroit he had two rushing touchdowns, including the game-winner. After the previous week, nobody should have been surprised when the Chiefs turned to Darrel Williams for a late touch-down. "When the football is in my hands, I'm going to go to work," he said. "I bring a lot to the table."

Darrel Williams went on the injured reserve list, which ended his season, in December after injuring his hamstring, so he didn't get to play in the postseason. But he had already done his part against the Ravens and the Lions to help the Chiefs garner wins on their way to the Super Bowl.

6

RECIPE FOR DEFEAT

"As a player your job is to execute, make plays, make the tackles that come your way, be in the right gaps, control your gap, and dominate your individual matchups. At the end of the day, you look at the film, and these are some of the things that we are not doing. You look at missed tackles and guys being able to squeak out the extra yards to convert on these early-down runs and stuff like that. We get to third down. It's third-and-one, third-and-two. It's no mystery what these teams are coming in here to do."

—Defensive end Frank Clark after the Kansas City Chiefs' uninspiring Week Five game against the Indianapolis Colts.

THE KANSAS CITY CHIEFS ENTERED Week Five against the Indianapolis Colts with a 4–0 record, but their season hadn't been perfect. They allowed two fourth-quarter touchdowns in the season opener to Jacksonville Jaguars quarterback Gardner Minshew, a rookie sixth-round draft pick. They had a big offensive second quarter in Week Two against the Oakland Raiders but didn't score in the second half. They almost wasted a 17-point, fourth-quarter lead against the Baltimore Ravens in Week Three. They needed a last-minute touchdown to beat the Detroit Lions in Week Four.

All of those troubles—offensive sluggishness and an inability to finish a game defensively—came back to visit them against the Colts. In the Colts' 19–13 victory, the Chiefs were pushed around up front on both sides of the ball, which allowed Indianapolis to dominate in number of plays (74–57) and time of possession (more than 37 minutes for the Colts and fewer than 23 minutes for the Chiefs).

To make matters worse the player who the Chiefs discarded in order to make room for Frank Clark came back to Arrowhead Stadium and dominated the game. Justin Houston made one of the game's biggest plays with about five minutes left and the Colts ahead 16–10. He tackled Damien Williams for a one-yard loss on a fourth-and-1 play, effectively ending the Chiefs' chances for a comeback. Houston also had a sack. Clark, meanwhile, failed to register a sack and at this point had one through five games. He had yet to become the player the Chiefs needed him to be when they released Houston and used a first-round pick to acquire him from the Seattle Seahawks. The game made it appear that the Chiefs had erred in making both moves.

Though the margin of defeat was just six points, the Chiefs were so dominated physically that it prompted some soul-searching on both sides of the ball. "Obviously, we didn't block," tackle Mitchell Schwartz said. "You can have the best quarterback in the world, the best receivers, and all that stuff, and it just doesn't matter when the guys are getting there too soon. We knew they had a good defensive line. We knew it would be a good challenge for us. Obviously, we didn't live up to expectations."

Meanwhile, the defense allowed 180 rushing yards for the third straight game. "Teams are going to do this every week to us until we figure it out," defensive back Tyrann Mathieu said. "They are going to run the ball down our throats. After a while it becomes a pride thing. It has nothing to do with coaching, it has nothing to do with technique. It has everything to do with attitude and if you want to stop it."

In an unusual and startling admission after the game, head coach Frank Reich said the Colts had been prepared to make some unorthodox maneuvers against the Chiefs because he thought they would be necessary to combat Kansas City's high-powered offense. That's how intimidating the thought was of facing Patrick Mahomes. But Reich found such moves weren't necessary because of the extent to which his team controlled the game. "All week long I was looking at the charts and talking to our analytics guys," Reich said. "We were prepared to do some crazy things like go for fourth downs being backed up and stuff like that. But we never really got into that situation. I talked about it with our staff. We were going to be aggressive but not reckless. I could tell the way our defense was playing. I had a good feeling they were going to play like that. We were never put in that situation. It was dictated by how our players played. We did not have to be reckless because they were playing good football."

For the Chiefs the loss could have been just a loss. They were still at this point 4–1. But the Colts game had some overtones that were ominous and indeed would be a problem for the Chiefs in their next game against the Houston Texans and some others through the middle of the season. The Colts designed what seemed to be the perfect gameplan for taking down Mahomes and the Chiefs.

Ball control: Indianapolis put a lot of pressure on the Chiefs by not only dominating snap counts and time of possession, but also by scoring on five of its nine drives. That didn't count the final drive when the Colts were running out the clock. The strategy was used the week before in the near upset by the Lions, who just didn't execute as well as the Colts did. The Texans would dominate the game the same way the next week in their win against the Chiefs. While the Chiefs allowed 180 rushing yards against the Colts, they had just 36 themselves, and Mahomes was sacked four times. The Chiefs had just four possessions in the second half. "I've got to get the bigs playing better," Andy Reid said, referring to the linemen on both offense and defense. "It starts there. When you win, it starts there. When you lose, it starts there, too."

Constant pressure on Mahomes: The Chiefs did a lousy job of protecting Mahomes, who was sacked four times and hit on several other occasions. The Chiefs allowed more sacks just once all season, and that came later in the season against the Minnesota Vikings when the less-mobile Matt Moore played at quarterback instead of the injured Mahomes. "We didn't block well," Schwartz said. "Your offense can't function when the o-line doesn't do its job. It doesn't matter how good [Mahomes] is, how good the receivers are, how good Kelce is, how good our running backs are. We've seen all these guys and what they can do [when given time]. You leave the game thinking your unit lost it for the team."

The Chiefs didn't try to relieve pressure by calling more running plays. They tried runs on just 14 of their 57 plays. LeSean McCoy, their leading rusher entering the game, got zero carries. "They were banged up a little bit in the secondary," Reid said of the Colts. "I thought we could take advantage of that."

The Chiefs weren't productive with the run, gaining 36 yards. A more concerted effort to run the ball might have made a difference.

Man-to-man coverage: This issue wasn't new for the Chiefs, but the Colts did a better job of it than many of Kansas City's other opponents had done. "Detroit did it last week," Mahomes said. "New England did it in the playoffs. We're going to have to beat man coverage at the end of the day. We've got the guys to do it. Now it's about going out there and executing whenever teams present it to us. If we don't, we're going to keep getting it."

Timing: The Chiefs lost Sammy Watkins to a hamstring injury on their first possession of the Colts game. That meant they played the rest way without either of their starters, as Tyreek Hill hadn't played since Week One. The Chiefs' leading receiver against the Colts was Byron Pringle, who caught six passes for 103 yards and one touchdown. Pringle, a second-year player out of Kansas State, had a previous career high of one catch for 13 yards. The Chiefs also played without left tackle Eric Fisher, who in September had surgery for a sports hernia. His replacement, Cam Erving, struggled to block Houston. Hill would return the following week against the Texans, but injuries on both sides of the ball would continue to be a problem for the Chiefs for the next few weeks.

Hobbled Mahomes: He sprained his ankle in the season opener against Jacksonville, and, though his injury hadn't been discussed much publicly because he has practiced and played, it was a problem for him. Mahomes threw incomplete to open receivers more often than he normally would. The ankle was a particular problem for Mahomes against the Colts. He aggravated the injury in the first half and again in the third quarter, when he was accidentally stepped on by a teammate. Mahomes at that point was limping noticeably. He was able to finish the game but wasn't as strong as he would have preferred.

The Chiefs scored fewer points against the Colts than they had in any start Mahomes had made for them. The previous low was 26. He had a lower QBR (50.5) against Indianapolis than in any game of his career to that point. During his first season as a starter in 2018, Mahomes became the second quarterback to throw 50 touchdown passes and for more than 5,000 yards. After gliding to another strong start in 2019—he threw 10 touchdown passes and for almost 1,200 yards in the first three games—the Chiefs quarterback found himself amidst the first real adversity of his pro career. "I've definitely been through adverse times when I was in college of not winning the games I felt like we could have won," he said. "There were certain times at

Texas Tech when we didn't do the things we wanted to as an offense to find ways to win. My first year here, the team went through a little stretch where they weren't winning games. It's a long season. You can figure it out. There are difficult times in the NFL. Teams are good, and we've played some great opponents so far this season, and we'll have to find a way to get this thing rolling again."

Mahomes had a game in 2018, in which he threw six touchdown passes and for almost 500 yards but also committed five turnovers that were costly in a 54–51 loss to the Los Angeles Rams. One of Mahomes' three interceptions and one of his two fumbles on that Monday night were returned for touchdowns. "You have to eliminate the turnovers," Mahomes said a few days after the Rams game. "Some of those turnovers came at crucial moments. I think the biggest one for me was the one where we were almost in field-goal range, just knowing when to and when not to take a chance. Every experience, bad or good, you have to learn from. You take the positives. We had a lot of successful plays and successful things that happened in that game, but you have to find ways to win them in the end."

Mahomes bounced back well from that game, throwing for 295 yards and four touchdowns without a turnover. "You don't hide it," Reid said. "You go back and evaluate it: how did those things happen and then how do you fix them so they don't happen again? So we've done that. One thing about Pat is that he doesn't make the same mistake twice. That's not been his M.O. here. I'm not worried about that. I want him to keep firing. Learn from your mistakes but keep firing."

The turnovers came at a cost of winning that game, but Mahomes learned some valuable lessons. One is that great pass rushers like Rams defensive tackle Aaron Donald, who forced both of the fumbles, aren't content with just a sack. They want the ball, too. Mahomes said after the game he felt Donald's presence each time but was surprised the pass rusher went for the ball as well as the quarterback.

He also threw an interception when he couldn't decide on which of his two receivers to throw the ball to. That was the interception that was returned for a touchdown. "You just have to be decisive," Mahomes said. "I was indecisive with the throw."

His struggles against the Colts were of a different variety. His sore ankle raised the question of whether the Chiefs would be better off putting Mahomes on the bench until his injury would allow him to play in his normal style and with his usual effectiveness. This was a notion that he, of course, pushed back on. "If I felt my ankle was affecting the team and the success of the offense, I would for sure move on," Mahomes said. "But at the same time, I feel like I'm still moving around. I'm still able to run, scramble, throw. I'm good now. I still get treatment and stuff like that, but I feel like I can still do everything I need to do."

The Chiefs were counting on it. "We're going to bounce back," Hill said. "We're the Chiefs. That's what we do. We've got the MVP quarterback."

7

DEFENSIVE GROWING PAINS

"We've got good character in that locker room all the way around. We've got to stay positive and upbeat with it and learn from the mistakes. That's what you've got to do. I've seen us play better, so that's my responsibility that we make sure we get to that position. But the character of this team is solid. We just have to flip a few things. The margin of winning and losing in this league is small. You're just a play or two away from coming out of this thing with a win, so we have to take care of business. That's what we have to do. Every season is going to give you some hurdles you'll have to scale, and this is one of those challenges. It tests you, but we'll bear down. We'll bear down and get it done."

—Andy Reid after the Chiefs' second straight defeat.

NEW DEFENSIVE COORDINATOR STEVE SPAGNUOLO had quite a task after being hired by the Kansas City Chiefs in the 2019 offseason. Among his duties to prepare for the upcoming season were to scrap the Chiefs' old 3-4 base system and replace it with a new 4-3, help Andy Reid hire the rest of the new defensive staff, get the new coaches all pointed in the same direction, and then teach the new system to the players, many of whom would be arriving in the coming weeks through free agency, the draft, or trade.

At times as the months rolled by, Spagnuolo could see signs of progress. At other moments he seemed overwhelmed by the process. But it appeared early in the season that the Chiefs went too far in their effort. They were still trying to work out their defensive issues after the 31–24 loss to the Houston Texans in Week Six. "As a staff, as a group of players and coaches, we're still trying to figure out what it is we do best, who fits where," Spagnuolo said. "There is still a little bit of that going on, and throughout the season, we'll be doing that."

Nobody disputed the Chiefs had to try something new on defense. In 2018 the Chiefs went 12–4, won the AFC West for the third straight year, and won a home playoff game for the first time in 25 years, but further success was wasted by the defense. In his first year as a starter, Patrick Mahomes threw for 5,000 yards and 50 touchdowns and won the league's MVP, but in the end, it counted for little when the defense collapsed in the AFC Championship Game against the New England Patriots.

But by Week Six—almost halfway through the season—the defense wasn't working as consistently as the Chiefs hoped. It had some good moments early in the season—for five consecutive quarters spanning games against the Oakland Raiders and Baltimore Ravens, the Chiefs allowed just six points, had two takeaways, and halted six drives at three or four plays before a punt—but just not enough of them.

They had few such good moments on defense against the Texans, who ran 83 plays. It's hard for a defense to succeed when the defense is on the field for that many snaps, and the Chiefs most definitely didn't. They allowed almost 40 minutes time of possession and almost 500 yards.

"It's very frustrating," defensive end Frank Clark said. "At the end of the day, those are more plays you are playing, unnecessary plays. You've got these opportunities to get off of the field and you might have a penalty that extends a drive or stuff like that we can control. That's self-inflicted. Not enough pressure on the quarterback. We didn't do our job as far as that. You've got these collaborative things that are going on all at the same time and you don't stop the run if you are not tackling. We have to get back to our aggression, our passion for stopping the run. As you can see, early in the season, after six weeks, we have not been able to do that. That's just being honest. Over 100 yards rushing every week against our opponents, some running backs are more well-known than others, but we are making everybody look awesome. We are making every running back we play look awesome. For the most part, the offenses we are playing, we haven't shut down an offense this year. That is something we have to do in order to win. We can't keep putting the pressure on our offense to do everything. We can't keep putting the pressure on those guys to get the job done. We know what they can do, but we've got to give them more opportunities. We've got to slow the game down on defense so we are not getting these extended drives, nine-play drives, 10-play drives."

Yardage figures are generally going to be inflated against the Chiefs, who held leads of at least 17 points in each of their first three games. But their inability to finish defensively in the season opener against the Jacksonville Jaguars, who scored 13 points in the fourth quarter, and against the Ravens, who scored 22 in the second half, had them frustrated. "We went into halftime with the Ravens having less than 10 points, and the game ended with 28 points," defensive lineman Chris

Jones said. "The rushing yards tripled after halftime. As a defense you don't like that. You kind of have to be consistent with it, especially on defense when you have the lead coming out of halftime. You want to put your foot on their throat and just dominate the game right there. I feel like we kind of let them back into the game. It's a new defense. That's the biggest challenge. I've been saying it all year. When you've got a new defense, there are a lot of challenges. It's not going to be perfect. You're going to fail wishing for that every time. There are still guys grasping the concept of where they need to be, where they need to fill, and exactly what job they exactly need to do."

Clark had an important third-down sack in the fourth quarter against the Ravens but otherwise had produced little through the first six weeks of the season, and this came a season after recording 13 sacks for the Seattle Seahawks. The Chiefs invested heavily in Clark, trading a first-round pick in 2019, a second-round pick in 2020, and also swapping third-round picks with Seattle in 2019 before giving him a five-year deal with more than $62 million guaranteed. "One thing I told myself I need to do a better job of is managing my reps," Clark said. "I see myself out there sometimes for 15 straight plays. And by the time I get to those opportunities where I need to go rush and I need some legs, I don't [have] it. That's just being honest."

Although that was disappointing for the Chiefs to hear from one of their top defenders and a player they had given up so much for in terms of draft picks and cash, the Chiefs braced for a difficult defensive transition early in the season. They came close to a complete rebuild during the offseason. It was a lot of change in a very short period, but the Chiefs thought they couldn't afford to wait. "It was a little ambitious and aggressive, but that's the mode we operate in," general manager Brett Veach said. "We have a great offense and we want to take advantage of that every year and while they're all young and healthy and playing at a high level. Offense, especially with Coach Reid, is an execution deal and it's timing and precision. It's reps upon reps upon reps. Not to say that defense isn't, but defense is more of a mind-set and a temperament. So you want to bring in guys that are going to come in and get other players to respond to them."

Mere hours after AFC Championship Game loss, Reid decided to turn over the defensive staff led by longtime coordinator Bob Sutton. He resisted a similar change the year before out of respect for Sutton's abilities and instead focused on fixing defensive problems by changing players. The Chiefs brought in five veterans and drafted defensive players with their first five picks. "Our first three, four years, I thought we were really good on defense," said Reid, who joined the Chiefs in 2013. "It kind of carried us for a little bit."

The 2018 defensive changes didn't work. The Chiefs got old on defense. They received almost nothing from safety Eric Berry, who was injured for most of a second straight season. The Chiefs finished 31st in total defense—ahead of only the 6–10 Cincinnati Bengals. "Unfortunately in this business, sometimes that happens," Reid said. "That transition sometimes just doesn't work. Sometimes change can be good. It can be healthy if handled the right way. Spags is a veteran coach. Bringing people in that worked with him or were familiar with his system was a good get there and important."

The Chiefs might not have attempted such bold defensive turnover if they were starting a staff from scratch. But Spagnuolo worked eight seasons for Reid as a defensive assistant with the Philadelphia Eagles. The Chiefs hired four other new defensive coaches. All had played or coached with Spagnuolo. "The good thing was that there was already a rapport between Spags and Andy," Veach said. "I had spent some time with Spags in Philly. So when he came in, we were speaking the same language and were able to effectively communicate."

The next step was a significant player overhaul. The Chiefs cleared out Berry and other longtime veterans such as Justin Houston, Allen Bailey, and Dee Ford, who had 13 sacks the previous season but was not viewed as a fit for the new system. Some players survived the purge, most notably Jones. With 15.5 sacks in 2018, Jones emerged as one of the NFL's top defensive linemen. Cleaning up an underperforming defensive roster was the easy part.

The Chiefs also had to add, and the first piece, Tyrann Mathieu, was costly. He signed for three years and $42 million, making him the highest-paid safety in the league at the time. To Veach, Mathieu was essential to the process. In Berry's absence the Chiefs suffered at safety. The team rated Mathieu higher than any of the other available free-agent safeties, including Earl Thomas and Landon Collins. From the moment he walked through the Arrowhead Stadium doors, Mathieu became the Chiefs' defensive leader, the player others looked to for guidance. "The expectations are high, especially with our football team, especially with the defense just trying to set a standard," Mathieu said. "It starts with Spags. He's won some championships. He's put some great players in the Hall of Fame with a few more to be inducted. The sky is the limit, but it's going to be a tough hill to climb. It won't be easy. It's a new scheme for all of us, so there's going to be some valleys in there. I think that's why I'm here: to kind of keep guys up, to keep their spirits right. I think we'll be all right."

After signing Mathieu, the Chiefs filled in with other defensive pieces: linebacker Damien Wilson, cornerback Bashaud Breeland, defensive ends Alex Okafor and Emmanuel Ogbah, and safety Juan Thornhill, a second-round draft pick. Their other major acquisition came in the days before the draft. The Chiefs kept an eye on Clark for months, identifying him as a possible free-agent addition. The Seahawks effectively kept him off the free-agent market by making him their franchise player. That necessitated a trade. "We were in dialogue with Seattle for a long time," Veach said. "They had some things they had to work through with Russell Wilson and Bobby Wagner. I felt the longer it went on, the more they were thinking about it. The dialogue early on was always, 'Let's stay in touch.' That was a positive sign to us, encouraging to us."

Veach wouldn't let a possible deal die. The trade was reached when the Chiefs sent first- and second-round picks to the Seahawks and signed Clark to a five-year contract worth more than $100 million. Clark played on a top five defense in his first two NFL seasons with the Seahawks in 2015 and '16. "The first step for the Chiefs is creating that competitive atmosphere," Clark said. "Just being brutally honest, it wasn't here on the defensive side last year. When you look around, you see total defense, and we ranked 31st in the league. That doesn't make anyone proud. As a fan, as a coach, as a player, you shouldn't be proud. We're coming in here with a whole different type of attitude. We're coming here to win, we're coming here to compete, and we want to be the best. It's just that time for the competitors to come out and compete and for everyone else to fall off."

The Chiefs finished the season with 45 sacks, putting them 11th in the league. But against the Texans they failed to get a sack for the second straight game, leaving doubts about where the Chiefs were headed. "You can't do everything," Veach said. "There are only so many picks you have and so much money you have. But we feel good about the things we were able to get done. We felt like Mathieu was the best safety out there, and Frank Clark was the best pass rusher out there. We utilized the resources we had the best way we could."

The Chiefs were encouraged by some early signs. Clark and Jones were a strong pass rushing tandem. Thornhill looked to be a bargain. The defense presented some problems to Mahomes and one of the NFL's best offenses during training camp. "They do a lot of stuff," Mahomes said after one training camp practice. "It is hard to read. They get me a good amount of times where I think I have them picked up and they have something that goes off of something they may have done two days earlier. Just having that inbox where they can go and show one blitz one day and then do the exact opposite the other day when it looks the same will be something that will be hard for other offenses to progress against."

Spagnuolo and the Chiefs raced to get the defense ready to start the season, but the coordinator had to simplify his plans early in the year. "That's something I have to make a real hard decision on," Spagnuolo said during the preseason. "It will be dictated by what the guys can do. I do believe that as you approach this thing, you'd better make sure that they're not thinking and that they're playing—if that makes any sense. I'm hoping we've got the kind of guys that can handle multiple defensive packages and still play fast, but we'll see."

Mathieu played his best game of the season against Baltimore. He broke up three passes and could have intercepted two of them. One came in the end zone on a play where he left the receiver he was covering to deflect a pass to another receiver. "Normally, he just plucks that thing and catches it," Spagnuolo said. "It would have been a completely different outcome had he caught a couple of those. The encouraging thing is we're there and able to possibly make the play. I've got complete confidence in Tyrann that he'll make those going forward. He typically does. Nobody is beating himself up more than him."

But Spagnuolo's system puts a premium on pressure and takeaways, so the Chiefs were expecting more. "We're so close," Reid said. "You see it. We're right there. We're getting our hands on the ball or we're hesitant in some areas to go get the ball. They're small things, but I look at that and I go, 'You give that a little time, and those things change.' Some of the guys have been in the league, and I've seen it before, so you know that's going to come. You saw Tyrann in position to make a couple interceptions. Those things happen. The more familiar you become with the defense, then you're not off by just that tick. Then you're even in better position. Then you just have to play. You have to keep going with it and you've got to keep attacking or it doesn't happen."

The Chiefs played their best defensive game of the season to date the next week against the Denver Broncos, but that was a footnote to what seemed at the time to be a much bigger development.

8

MAHOMES' SCARY KNEE INJURY

"Not too many people get hurt on sneaks. It was a freak thing; sometimes it happens. I was really proud of how our guys stepped up and didn't let themselves down. You've seen that over the years where teams let themselves down when one of your best players get hurt, particularly the quarterback. But I was proud of how our guys stepped up and just kept battling. I thought they really upped their game."

—Andy Reid on whether he regretted calling a quarterback sneak that resulted in a knee injury to Patrick Mahomes.

KANSAS CITY CHIEFS GUARD LAURENT DUVERNAY-TARDIF is a medical school graduate from Montreal's McGill University and specialized in emergency medicine there. After experiencing many emergency room shifts, he's been hardened to seeing traumatic injuries. But he still acknowledged being stunned by what he saw of Patrick Mahomes' knee in the second quarter of a Thursday night, Week Seven game against the Broncos in Denver. Following a quarterback sneak, Mahomes' right knee had been so horribly pushed out of place that the kneecap was on the side of the joint instead of the front.

Duvernay-Tardif didn't need any vast medical knowledge to realize Mahomes and by extension the Chiefs' Super Bowl hopes were in some trouble. "Everybody could have known something was wrong," Duvernay-Tardif said. "He was saying, 'It's out, it's out.' Nobody really understood what he meant at that time, and then we saw it. That's when we started panicking. Not panicking but seeing that he was not all right."

Mahomes dislocated the patella. It was quickly massaged back into place by members of the Chiefs' medical staff, but he left the game at that point and didn't return. "His knee didn't even look like a knee," Travis Kelce said. "It was all out of whack. I couldn't even describe it."

That made the incident doubly difficult for Mahomes' teammates. They saw the grotesque nature of the injury, which happened on a seemingly innocent play, and felt for their fallen teammate. On some level each also considered what a long-term injury might mean for the larger group and their season. Some of the developments in the moments after the injury offered hope that Mahomes would be able to return sooner rather than later. The medical staff acted quickly to restore Mahomes' kneecap to its proper place, which helped accelerate Mahomes' recovery.

A motorized cart came on to the field to take Mahomes away for diagnosis, but he refused it and was helped off the field by a couple of trainers as players from both teams came by to offer encouragement. Mahomes soon left for the locker room, walking under his own power but with a limp. The Chiefs quickly said he would not play again that night. Mahomes addressed his teammates in the locker room after the game, a 30–6 victory, with his leg in a black sleeve. He appeared in good spirits as he slapped hands with teammates. "Take care of yourself this weekend," Mahomes said to his teammates, who wouldn't have another game for 10 days. "Enjoy yourself. Be smart. We got more to go, baby."

The Chiefs did an X-ray of Mahomes' knee after the game, and it came back negative. He had an MRI the following day after the Chiefs returned to Kansas City, and the injury turned out, according to head athletic trainer Rick Burkholder, "as good as we could possibly imagine."

Perhaps the best indication that Mahomes' absence wouldn't be an extended one came the day after the game when he started the rehab process with therapy in a swimming pool.

The Chiefs got through the remainder of the Denver game with veteran backup Matt Moore replacing Mahomes. A career journeyman with 30 starts for the Carolina Panthers and Miami Dolphins, the 35-year-old Moore joined the Chiefs at the end of training camp. He had never played in a game for the Chiefs and hadn't done so for any team—even in the preseason—for two seasons.

The Chiefs led 10–7 at the time of Mahomes' injury and held off the Broncos more with the strong play of their defense than anything else. They had nine sacks and scored a defensive touchdown. Their only offensive touchdown with Moore came when he beat a Denver blitz by throwing a 57-yard touchdown pass to Tyreek Hill, who was the only regular Chiefs receiver to have much familiarity with Moore. Their bond came on the scout team earlier in the season when the injured Hill was preparing for his eventual return against the Houston Texans. "I had a chance to go against the defense, and he was the quarterback," Hill said. "We were out there drawing up plays. I was Will Fuller; he was Deshaun Watson. Me and him, we kind of got a connection going."

Moore made no mistakes against the Broncos that cost the Chiefs. But other than his touchdown pass to Hill, it was difficult to be optimistic about what his team could accomplish offensively without Mahomes as the quarterback. Andy Reid took some criticism for opting to use Mahomes to sneak on the fourth-down play, which he converted. "Not too many people get hurt on a sneak," Reid said after the game. "It's a freak thing, and it happens."

But the Chiefs didn't run a quarterback sneak the remainder of the season.

The injury was the most significant of three during the season for Mahomes. It would take him out of the lineup for the second half in Denver and the subsequent two games, which were both against eventual playoff teams, the Green Bay Packers and the Minnesota Vikings.

Mahomes entered the Denver game hobbled by a left ankle injury. He sprained the ankle in the Week One game against the Jacksonville Jaguars and aggravated it at various points leading up to the Denver game. But he played through it and intended to do so against the Broncos. In that sense having to miss the Packers and Vikings games may have been the best thing for Mahomes. "The ankle is good," he said after returning to the lineup later in the season. "We knew we needed rest for the ankle. We knew we needed some days off. With having the knee, I got to rest that ankle. I was able to play and do what could. I don't have any pain there."

Mahomes, as things turned out, missed no practice time. After the Thursday night game in Denver, the Chiefs had a few days off, and Mahomes was able to practice by the time they regrouped for work the following Monday. He was a limited practice participant, but the Chiefs still quickly got the sense Mahomes' absence wouldn't be an extended one.

Nobody knew that in the immediate aftermath of the Denver game. The thought at the time was that the Chiefs would have to go as far as they could with Moore as their quarterback. They did their best to put a happy face on that prospect. Mahomes gathered his teammates in the postgame locker room and lauded Moore by shouting, "How about my guy?" His teammates cheered.

Kelce soon urged the Chiefs to rally around Moore. "Matty came in full of energy and ready to rock and roll," Kelce said. "Matty Moore is 1–0."

Duvernay-Tardif could have treated Mahomes' injury on the field, though he left it to the medical professionals on the Chiefs' training staff. Four years after being drafted by the Chiefs in the sixth round, he graduated medical school in 2018. That made him the rare NFL player to graduate from med school during his professional football career. To illustrate the dual life he lived as a med student and football player, Duvernay-Tardif allowed himself to attend the graduation ceremony and spend a few hours afterward with friends and family, but the celebration didn't last long. He soon returned to Kansas City to rejoin his teammates for offseason practice. "It's been eight years that I've been working for that moment," Duvernay-Tardif said. "Since the day I got drafted, I promised myself I was going to finish my studies and get that M.D. while I was still playing. It's one of those life projects that you promise yourself you're going to accomplish. But right now football is my main priority. I want to focus and see how good I can be. I'm putting medicine on hold in order to really maximize my opportunity in the NFL. I love playing football. For all of those who sometimes doubt that I really want to be here because I've got a medical degree, having a really strong Plan B and still playing football shows how much I really love the game. I love being out there with the guys. I love the chemistry we have in the locker room. Being out there is a privilege."

In this sense graduating from med school changed little for Duvernay-Tardif. He went back and forth between football and medical studies during college as well as when he joined the Chiefs. He lifted weights and stayed in football shape in the offseason while studying medicine in Montreal and he read medical journals after practice during the football season. "I'm never too far from medicine when I'm in K.C. and I'm never too far from football when I'm studying medicine," he said. "I have to stay in shape for football year-round and I have to stay up to date with medicine year-round."

Duvernay-Tardif's two worlds collided during the 2015 season. He had postponed a med school exam on orthopedic surgery the previous summer because he had to report to training camp. His test was rescheduled for the Chiefs' bye week in November—or four days after the team played the Detroit Lions in London. "I tried to study for that exam leading up to the bye, but I wasn't able to do it because I had so much football on my plate," he said. "So as soon as we jumped on the plane after that Detroit game, everybody else was partying on the plane, and I had my headset on. I was just studying, studying, studying. We got back to K.C. at 3:00 in the morning. We had a 30-minute meeting with Coach Reid. He cut us loose around 4:00. I took a cab straight back to the airport. I took the first flight out at 6:00 AM for Montreal, flew back to Montreal, and studied the whole way back. As soon as I landed in Montreal, I slept two hours, studied two hours, slept two hours, studied two hours for three days straight. I passed the exam at 61 percent or 63 percent. It was borderline, but I passed it. It was a pass-or-fail exam. I was so pumped. I slept for two days and then flew back to Kansas City. That was my bye week."

The Chiefs were initially skeptical about Duvernay-Tardif's commitment to football until they met with him before the 2014 draft. Reid and then-offensive coordinator Doug Pederson asked why a future doctor wanted to play football. "When you talked to him, you got the sense he was focused in and going," Reid said. "He wanted to play. He's got a love for it. He loves that part of it and he loves [the medical] part of it. You got that when you talked to him. I felt very comfortable about that when I talked to him. The way he's wired is just different. He's brilliant, but he can just get down and just be dirty tough. He's able to separate that. We're always talking about players and their life after football, which we encourage that you work on. So if you're going to be a doctor, you're going to have to spend a little extra time doing that. Then, hopefully you're driven enough when you come back to the football that you catch up and get where you need to be in order to play."

It probably didn't hurt that Reid's mother, Elizabeth, was a medical school graduate who also went to McGill. "The Chiefs saw it that I was playing football because I loved the game," Duvernay-Tardif said. "Otherwise, I wouldn't be here. For them knowing I was able to manage both at the same time in college was a positive thing. They knew when I was going to be in K.C., I was going to have a perfect work ethic. I was going to stay later, I was going to watch film."

He was seen as an oddity by his teammates the first time he walked into the Chiefs' locker room. "The first thing I heard from another offensive lineman was from Donald Stephenson," Duvernay-Tardif said. "He said, 'If I was a doctor, I wouldn't be here. Why are you here?' He didn't understand. Donald was the one who said that to me, but I think the other guys were a little bit asking themselves that question."

Duvernay-Tardif had to prove his football commitment to his teammates before he did so with coaches. One way he tried is by playing to the whistle and sometimes beyond even in practice. When there's a scuffle at practice, Duvernay-Tardif is inevitably involved. "The way I play, I go all out all the time," he said. "It's always 100 percent. When guys saw me on the field getting after it until the end of the whistle, they're like, 'okay, we've got a lot of respect for that guy.' When you get on the field and show toughness, your teammates feed off that and respect that."

Duvernay-Tardif was used to living the double life as a med student and football player when he joined the Chiefs because he lived that way in college. Knowing that medical school was at the time his priority, McGill's coaches accommodated Duvernay-Tardif's academic schedule. He was allowed to miss some meetings and practice sessions as long as he was available to play in games. During his college football seasons, Duvernay-Tardif was required to be at local hospitals at varying hours as part of his curriculum. "I tried to make practice as often as I could," he said. "Sometimes I would get off a shift, and practice was a few hours later. I would just head over to the locker room by the practice field, take a bunch of towels, put them on the floor, and go to sleep right there. The next morning my teammates would wake me up. They'd kick me in the ribs and tell me it was time to get to practice."

Duvernay-Tardif didn't play for the Chiefs as a rookie in 2014 but broke into the starting lineup the next season. He said he believes medical school helped him in football just as football helped him become a doctor. "You can do all the right things in football and still not earn a victory," he said. "In football you learn that sometimes you lose even while you're excellent. In medical school sometimes it's really hard for people to learn how to lose. Sometimes you're going to lose the battle in medical school. I remember the first time I did CPR on somebody who died. I think I was prepared to live that moment more than somebody who only had like straight As in med school and saw that for the first time. In football you learn to deal with tough situations."

With the injury to Mahomes, the Chiefs were going through a tough situation after the Broncos game. But things wouldn't be as bleak for them as they envisioned that night—thanks in large part to their temporary starter and the coaching he was receiving from Reid.

9

MATT MOORE TO THE RESCUE

"Of course, we are more comfortable with Pat out there, but we had a whole week to practice with him. I honestly feel he played well. We've got to execute better at every level of our playing field. We just have to get better and come out and fight harder and scratch hard to get the win…It's not just on Matt. It's on the offensive line, tight ends, and receivers to make his job easier. His job is to control the game and help us win the game, but it also has to do with the special teams, defense. We all have to make plays. We can't just single out and say, 'Matt, Matt, Matt' and make it about Matt. It's a whole team effort."

—Sammy Watkins on playing with Matt Moore at quarterback rather than the injured Patrick Mahomes against the Green Bay Packers.

NO FORMAL INTRODUCTIONS WERE NECESSARY when Matt Moore replaced Patrick Mahomes as the starting quarterback in a Week Eight game against the Green Bay Packers at Arrowhead Stadium. But Moore needed to acquaint himself with the Kansas City Chiefs receivers in a football sense. Moore joined the Chiefs as a backup at the end of training camp after veteran reserve Chad Henne injured his ankle. As the No. 2 quarterback in the regular season, Moore practiced only with the backups and not the regulars like Travis Kelce.

"I'm pretty sure three or four of the guys out there on the field had never caught a ball by Matt even in practice," Kelce said after Moore replaced the injured Mahomes in the previous week's game against the Denver Broncos. "I know I hadn't. It was just going out there and playing within the rules of the offense and trusting the guy to be able to put the ball somewhere."

Moore, Kelce, and the rest of the Chiefs offensive players got things down by the time they faced the Packers. The Chiefs quickly fell behind 14–0, but aided by two touchdown passes from Moore, they rallied to take a lead by halftime. The Chiefs eventually lost 31–24 to fall to 5–3. But Moore, who threw for 267 yards, stood toe to toe with Aaron Rodgers and kept the Chiefs in the game until the end.

Moore came up with another big game the following week against the Minnesota Vikings. The Chiefs won 26–23 on a walk-off field goal after Moore threw for 275 yards, making him a crucial part of Kansas City's Super Bowl season. If the Chiefs didn't win at least one of their two games while Mahomes was out of the lineup with a knee injury, they wouldn't have gotten a first-round playoff bye. That would have meant a three-game path for the Chiefs to the Super Bowl. As things turned out, they instead needed just two games to get to Miami, and both of them were played at Arrowhead.

When the Chiefs were looking for a backup quarterback to Mahomes in 2018, they looked at Moore but instead signed Henne. As they began training camp in 2019, Moore was nowhere on the Chiefs' radar except on their quarterback emergency list—the one all teams keep in a drawer in case injuries wreck their depth chart.

Moore was helping coach his former high school team in the Los Angeles area, thinking his NFL career, which at that point had spanned 11 years, could be finished. He had sat out the 2018 season, so he was looking at two seasons without playing until the Chiefs called. "Sitting out last year was great, but this training camp rolled around, and the juices kind of started flowing a little bit, but I really didn't expect a call," Moore said. "Sure, there were some thoughts that this may never happen. And then when it happens, you're like, 'Hey, let's go.' It's really that simple. I was out running around with the kids, and it was good. I didn't think [an NFL team would call again]. I thought it was over. I just got a phone call. Out of the blue, I got a phone call. I went about it quickly and made a decision. There was no plan. We weren't doing anything to find a job—if you will. It just kind of happened.

"It was kind of funny because I was super excited to sign here. Then once I got here, I was like, 'Holy smokes!' I had no camp, no [offseason practices], no nothing, and there's always that potential case where you have to play soon. That was always in my mind the first couple weeks. I just rely on the history and the experience that I have had in this league. I've always been the guy typically most of my career, who, yeah, I had training camp and all that stuff, but the reps haven't been there. Practice hasn't been there. As a backup that just doesn't happen. That's everywhere. I just kind of relied on that it's football, and it's concepts. You know what you're doing and go play. It's challenging, for sure. Lean on the people here and work hard. That's all you can do."

Moore came out of college at Oregon State in 2007 after going undrafted. So he already had exceeded expectations for his career by the time he joined the Chiefs. Mostly for bad teams with the Carolina Panthers and Miami Dolphins, he made 30 starts and won half of them. This time, however, Moore was playing for a Super Bowl-contending team. He had followed the Chiefs closely in his season out of football in part because he had almost landed a job there but also because of what Mahomes and the Chiefs were accomplishing offensively. "How could you not pay attention to them?" He said. "It was incredible. Obviously, Coach Reid has an incredible history with teams, offenses, players…Anybody would be excited to be here."

He finished the Denver game in place of Mahomes, and his 57-yard touchdown pass to Tyreek Hill helped break the game open. The Chiefs would have beaten the Broncos without that play. But they needed Moore to make some plays against the Packers particularly after they had fallen behind early, and he delivered. He unloaded just before Green Bay's pass rush reached him to throw a 29-yard touchdown pass to Kelce. He also threw a 30-yard touchdown pass to Mecole Hardman, who was running a jet sweep in front of Moore. All Moore had to do was flip the ball to Hardman.

Regardless of how long he had been around, Moore gave the Chiefs more in his two starts than they any right to expect from the journeyman backup. One of his career highlights came against the Chiefs in 2011. He threw for 244 yards and three touchdowns and had a career-best passer rating of 147.5 in the Dolphins' 31–3 victory.

Andy Reid had been good throughout his coaching career at preparing backups like Moore in emergency situations like this and often on short notice. So he knew exactly how to tweak his gameplan for Moore. "I don't think we'll have to change the whole offense, but definitely, sure," Reid said. "That's part of being a coach and knowing your players. You want to put them in the best position for what they do so you can utilize those tools there. It's not going to be exactly like Pat. They're all different. We've got enough in the offense where I might be able to get [Moore] a couple of plays. He's got ice water in his veins. He doesn't flinch, and there's no panic. He says, 'I'm good, just call it, and let's roll.' It's hard to do, really, the whole thing he's done here, coming in late to us when Chad got hurt, and then asking him to pick up this offense, which is pretty complicated. He's a pro and he's done a very nice job with it. It's hard to be a relief pitcher, but he's done it before, and there's a certain way to prep for that. He understands that, and it paid off for him. The best part is we didn't have to change up a lot of things. The hard thing to do is if one guy comes in, the backup comes in, and you have to change the whole offense right away. That's a tough deal. We didn't have to do that with him."

The Chiefs had to turn to backup quarterbacks in earlier seasons with Reid. Chase Daniel was 1–1, but only a missed field-goal attempt in the final seconds kept him from being undefeated. Nick Foles was 1–0 as a starter in Kansas City. Mahomes was 1–0 during his rookie season. Going back to Reid's time with the Philadelphia Eagles, many of the backup quarterbacks had a winning record in replacing the injured Donovan McNabb. Jeff Garcia went 5–1, A.J. Feeley went 4–3, and Koy Detmer went 2–1.

Going with a backup quarterback doesn't usually mean defeat for Reid. Feeley, who started for Reid in two different stays with the Eagles in 2002 and 2007, said Reid is better at tailoring his gameplans to accentuate a quarterback's strengths and minimize his weaknesses than any coach he played for in his other two NFL stops. "I wouldn't say he necessarily makes playing the position easier, but he puts every quarterback in the best spot to be successful," Feeley said. "That's not always the case for coaches around the league or schemes. He's just got the knack for getting you in the right play so you're not behind the eight ball to begin with. He's good at giving guys the short passing game and easier reads to kind of get into the flow of a game. That's helpful to any quarterback but really to a quarterback who hasn't played a lot recently. I've been on other teams where it's a vertical passing game, and it's your job to make it work without a lot of tutelage on what they really want. With Andy you go into it prepared."

Feeley said Reid gives his quarterbacks an unusual amount of input into the gameplan. The day before every game, Reid calls the quarterbacks into a meeting to collect their favorite plays for various situations: first down, goal line and short yardage, third down, red zone, etc. "Andy will meet with Matt during the week, probably on Saturday morning, to kind of go over what he likes in terms of the gameplan." Feeley said. "I imagine if there's a question in the game of running one play or the other, knowing what Matt is more comfortable with, he will call that one."

Feeley joined the Eagles as a fifth-round draft pick in 2001, but he had to start five games the next season because of injuries to the Eagles' other quarterbacks. "When I first had to play, I was young and really inexperienced," Feeley said. "The first couple of games, he might have called the game to that and allowed me to have success and allowed him to see if I could handle it. The first game or two were run-heavy in terms of the gameplan. He didn't know if I could handle it. As we went on, he opened it up to the full offense, knowing I could handle it. From the point I was made the starter, Andy didn't flinch. There was no hesitation. He didn't waver. There was no hand-holding. He told me he had expectations for me just like he had for Donovan but that he would help me reach those expectations just like he did for Donovan. There's an aura about Andy that's hard to describe. He's not a big talker, but he asks a lot of questions. With me when I first started to play, he only gave me things he thought I was good at and that he thought we'd be successful at. He didn't just throw me out there and tell me to make things happen. That takes a lot of stress off a quarterback's shoulders. He played to my strengths and—once he realized how comfortable I was becoming and that I could do more things—he started to open up the playbook accordingly. As a quarterback there are certain variables that go into your ability to be successful. One of the major ones is the offense you run and the guy calling the plays."

By the time he replaced Mahomes in Denver, Moore had gone almost two years without playing in a game. His previous game action occurred on November 26, 2017, when he threw for 215 yards, one touchdown, and two interceptions for the Dolphins in a 35–17 loss to the New England Patriots. "I've played in this league before," he said. "Just like everybody I've had my ups and downs. It's been a wild half a year or whatever. You've just got to move forward and go."

He put his experience to use and figured some things out against the Broncos. He knew of Hill's speed—he told himself not to leave the throw short on the touchdown pass—and made a nice throw by lofting the ball over a defender who was in the passing lane. Against the Vikings he threw to Hill on the game-winning drive for 13 yards to allow the Chiefs to convert on third and 4. The Vikings got early pressure, which both Moore and Hill recognized. They made adjustments. Hill shortened his route, and Moore got rid of the ball quickly. "Early on you get to watch and you try to pick up as much as you can about these guys and their style of play and how they play," Moore said. "So I had that benefit from just watching him for a little bit and then obviously being with him from the past couple of weeks. You get to know quickly because it can benefit you as a quarterback. I had anticipated that he was going to recognize that and quicken up, and that's exactly what he did. It was a big play for us."

New England Patriots running back Rex Burkhead scores the overtime touchdown to defeat the Chiefs in the 2018 AFC Championship Game. That loss proved to be a major source of motivation for Kansas City.

Head coach Andy Reid (left) and general manager Brett Veach (right) announce the signing of defensive back Tyrann Mathieu. That acquisition was instrumental in the defense's improvement.

While losing their second straight game in a home defeat to the Houston Texans, the Chiefs' run defense continued to struggle to contain running backs like Carlos Hyde.

Patrick Mahomes' knee injury, following a quarterback sneak versus the Denver Broncos, looked catastrophic at first.

While filling in for the injured Patrick Mahomes, quarterback Matt Moore throws a pass during his impressive performance against the Minnesota Vikings.

During his breakout performance, defensive end Frank Clark sacks quarterback Philip Rivers to help the Chiefs defeat the Los Angeles Chargers in Mexico City.

Quarterbacks Patrick Mahomes and Tom Brady speak after the Chiefs defeated the New England Patriots to perhaps signal a changing of the guard in the AFC.

Travis Kelce catches one of his 11 passes in the snowy 23–3 victory against the
Denver Broncos to become the first tight end in NFL history with four straight
1,000-yard receiving seasons.

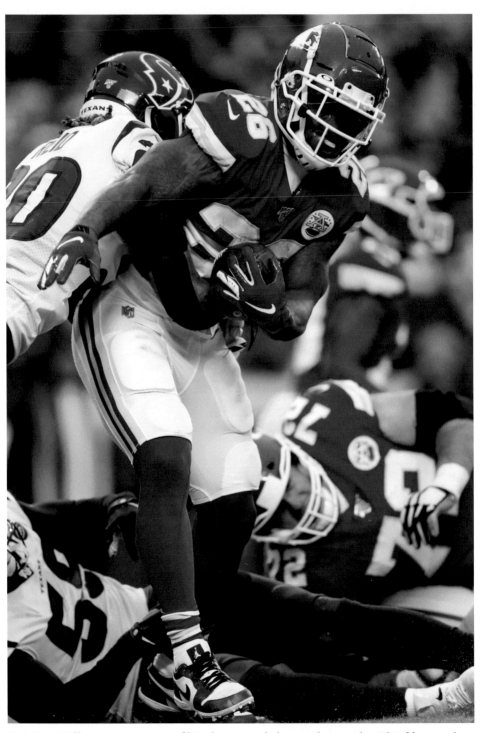

Damien Williams scores one of his three touchdowns during the Chiefs' remarkable comeback victory against the Houston Texans after trailing 24–0 in the divisional playoff round.

Patrick Mahomes raises the Lamar Hunt Trophy after the Chiefs defeated the Tennessee Titans 35–24 in the AFC Championship Game.

Right before he gets hit by DeForest Buckner, Patrick Mahomes throws a 44-yard completion to Tyreek Hill on third and 15, which will go down in Super Bowl lore.

Andy Reid and the Chiefs celebrate their 31–20 victory in Super Bowl LIV.

10

CHEETAH SPEED

"We are just trying to get that bad taste out of our mouths. I thought we played the game the right way today. I thought guys stepped up in a tough situation and made some big plays...Hopefully, it gets us rolling. We have been doing a lot of good things defensively. We have been trying to see those things stack up and carry over into the next week, week after week. I thought today we played pretty well against a really good offensive team that can really run the ball and set up deep play-action passes. I thought we did a good job of competing each and every down and trying to get off of the field on third down. I think when it mattered the most we stepped up and made the play."

—Tyrann Mathieu after the Kansas City Chiefs' comeback against the Minnesota Vikings in Week Nine.

ALL THE BUZZ SURROUNDING TYREEK HILL after the Kansas City Chiefs' 26–23 win against the Minnesota Vikings in Week Nine seemed to be about how he sprinted down the field to catch up and pass teammate Damien Williams on the running back's 91-yard touchdown run. It was an impressive play. According to NFL Next Gen Stats data, Hill hit a top speed of 22.64 mph—the fastest speed by a wide receiver during the 2019 regular season—on the play.

But Hill did so much more that mattered to the outcome that day. The Chiefs outlasted the Vikings, winning on Harrison Butker's 44-yard field goal as time expired. But they won because Hill was the best player on the field. Hill had multiple remarkable moments, including when he caught a 41-yard pass by tracking the ball better than cornerback Trae Waynes and then outmuscling his defender to make the catch. "He would have been a great center fielder," Andy Reid said. "He's got a unique combination [of skills]. The thing that amazes me the most is he's fast and quick, but it's his endurance being fast and quick. Normally, you don't see that. I tell him he's got this 'Cheetah' nickname, but he's really not a cheetah. They have a burst and they go rest for about eight hours. That's not this guy. He can keep going over and over again. It's pretty amazing."

Often one of the best players on the field during Chiefs games, Hill was essential to their success in 2019. He was a distant second to Travis Kelce in catches with 58 because he missed four games with an injury to his sternum and collarbone but still led the Chiefs in receiving touchdowns with seven.

It's easy to forget now, but before the season started, it didn't look like Hill would be available to play for the Chiefs in 2019—and perhaps ever again. Hill was investigated by the Johnson County (Kansas) District Attorney's office for possible child abuse after police were called twice to his home in March and determined Hill's three-year-old son had been injured.

The DA's office declined to press charges, saying, though it believed a crime had occurred, the evidence didn't establish who committed it.

Then a Kansas City TV station aired a portion of an audiotape, in which Hill and his then-fiancee, Crystal Espinal, discussed the boy's injuries, and Espinal seemed to blame Hill for inflicting them. Upon the airing of the audio, the Chiefs suspended Hill from offseason conditioning and practice, and general manager Brett Veach issued an ominously worded statement. "We were deeply disturbed by what we heard," Veach said. "We were deeply concerned. Now, obviously, we have great concern for Crystal. We are greatly concerned for Tyreek. But our main focus, our main concern, is with the young child."

The Chiefs' next action also seemed to suggest they were ready to move on from Hill. The day after the tape became public, the Chiefs drafted speedy wide receiver Mecole Hardman in the second round, trading up to get him. Later, a Kansas City radio station aired an additional portion of the audiotape of the discussion between Hill and Espinal. Hill denied committing assault and battery against Espinal in the earlier case despite his guilty plea.

Charges weren't filed in the child abuse case. Shortly before training camp started, the NFL announced it would take no action against Hill in the case, and the Chiefs lifted his suspension. His status for the 2019 season had quickly changed. "It's going to be awesome to welcome him back and bring him back with the guys and get to work," Patrick Mahomes said. "I'm happy that we get to welcome him back, and he will be there at training camp, and we can build that chemistry for the season."

Speaking publicly for the first time since being investigated, Hill said he needed to work on his life skills, though he didn't elaborate. "I can't wait for my new journey," Hill said. "I'm trying to grow each and every day of my life. To come back out here and to get a chance, it's crazy. I'm back. The Cheetah is back."

Before joining the Chiefs, Hill pleaded guilty in Oklahoma to punching and kicking a then-pregnant Espinal in 2015. It was one reason he was available to the Chiefs in the fifth round of the 2015 draft. The Chiefs drafted Hill amidst a flurry of questions about his past and whether the team thoroughly investigated Hill before drafting him and how seriously they took the charges against him. "We would never put anybody in this community in harm's way," the Chiefs' general manager at the time, John Dorsey, said after the Chiefs drafted Hill. "I have young children. I have a girl and I have a boy. I would hope that somebody in my seat did as much work as I. I would be happy with that. I know that I would never put this community in any type of situation where it would not be good, and we've done that. This is not about touchdowns. This is not about football. I understand it's about people and lives and communities. I understand that…we have done a lot of research within this thing. And that's where I'm coming from as the man and the person. We wouldn't bring a bad person here, and I've said that repeatedly for four drafts now. I won't do that. And if I felt like this was a bad person, I would not bring that person in. We have done a lot of research, we've turned over a lot of stones, and at the end of the day, this is not a bad person."

Reid had been through another controversial acquisition during his days coaching the Philadelphia Eagles. "There is a human element involved. I went through this with Michael Vick. He was really under the gun just like this, and all eyes were on him," Reid said. "He tried to come out of prison and tried to right the wrong. I saw that and I was sensitive to it, gave him a second chance. He's been one of the greatest things ever to happen to anti-dog fighting. He's been on a mission to try to help stop that. Somewhere, there's a human element like that that's involved. Sometimes people get caught up in things that are a little rough and tough and that you have to work through. Every situation is different. You really have to study, see the person, see the heart involved in that person. We think there will be a positive end to this. I just ask that we all let the young man get on with his work and his life and help encourage him. If we can get a positive out of this, that's great for humanity just itself, and then whatever he does on the football field is icing on the cake. I think it can be a win-win, bringing him to this great city of Kansas City. The people here are phenomenal, and I just look forward to them supporting him and giving him the encouragement that he needs to be a successful human being."

Away from the football field, Hill's first three seasons with the Chiefs were mostly uneventful. Before the latest child-abuse investigation, the Chiefs were planning to sign Hill to a long-term contract extension. The criminal investigation delayed the deal, but shortly before the start of the 2019 regular season, the Chiefs gave Hill a three-year contract extension worth $54 million.

Other than to acknowledge it, the Chiefs didn't address Hill's contract extension until the week of the Super Bowl. "His first year with us, there were some question marks coming into the league," chairman Clark Hunt said when the Chiefs were in Miami preparing for their game against the San Francisco 49ers. "We never had any issues with him. He always was where he was supposed to be, doing what he was supposed to be doing, accountable to the team, listening to his coaches, [being] a good teammate. I think we've seen that grow the last three or four years. Certainly, I sense a heightened level of maturity from him this year, which is probably a byproduct of the challenges he went through earlier this year. Part of it was our experience with him over the four years he had been with us. We knew him as an individual. We clearly wanted as much information as possible from the legal proceedings that were going on. We wanted to make sure he was in a good place emotionally, and that there weren't going to be any more surprises down the road…People in the organization would tell you that he's an outstanding father."

Between the reprieves from the legal system and the NFL and the new contract, Hill had some momentum heading into the season. It was removed in the first quarter of the season opening game when Jacksonville Jaguars cornerback Jalen Ramsey tackled Hill hard. The result was an unusual injury, one to his collarbone and sternum. He stayed the night in a Jacksonville hospital before returning to Kansas City.

Hill didn't return until a Week Six game against the Houston Texans and scored a touchdown on a 46-yard catch in the Chiefs' first drive of the game. He later made another touchdown reception that day. Hill calls himself "Cheetah" and calls his top gear "Cheetah speed." It's not just self-promotion. He may well be the NFL's fastest player. He ran a 4.24 in the 40 when he was coming out for the draft.

Hill was one of the NFL's top punt and kickoff return specialists until the Chiefs largely removed him from that duty to save wear and tear. He has five career return touchdowns, and 2019 was the first season that he didn't bring a kick back for a score. He had only a handful of chances. The Chiefs would send him out to return occasionally, mostly when they needed a big play. Such an instance happened late in the fourth quarter against the Vikings. With the score tied and 1:55 remaining, Minnesota's Britton Colquitt, the brother of the Chiefs' punter, punted to Hill from the Vikings' 18. Perhaps fearful of a long return, Colquitt sent his kick out of bounds at the Minnesota 45. From there the Chiefs needed just three plays—the biggest being a third-down catch by Hill—to get into field-goal range for Butker and his winning kick.

Hill can have that kind of effect on the opposition. Other teams sometimes observe Hill with a measure of awe. "That guy, Tyreek Hill, is unbelievable to watch," Los Angeles quarterback Philip Rivers said after a Chiefs victory against the Chargers. "What a dynamic player. I don't know if I've seen anybody better—the things he can do speed-wise—in all my time playing."

Even Hill's coaches and teammates are sometimes surprised by how fast he moves. "He's one of the fastest human beings I've ever seen line up in a pair of cleats," said Chiefs offensive coordinator Eric Bieniemy, a former NFL player and longtime assistant coach. "There's only been a few of them that I've looked back and said, 'Wow.' One being Deion Sanders. Rocket Ismail. When you have a player that has that unique gift to take the top off everything, yes, it does lighten the load for a lot of different people.'"

Another of the Chiefs' speedy receivers, Sammy Watkins, has 4.43 speed. "I'm fast," Watkins said. "But he's superfast."

Hill prides himself on his speed, but his game only starts there. "I've made my name in the NFL as being one of the fastest players, but right now I'm focusing on being one of the best at my craft," Hill said. "I want to be the best receiver.'"

Hill spends some time each offseason in Nebraska working with former Cornhuskers receivers coach Keith Williams on his route running, and Hill believes it is time well spent. "He taught me about the game, how it's played, how to be a complete receiver," Hill said. "I listened and I learned. I'm a quick learner."

If he's not the NFL's best receiver, Hill at least belongs in the discussion. His speed is only one reason. His knowledge of how to use it is another. "He is the fastest guy that's been in this league for a while," Watkins said. "He definitely has unique speed. You hear everybody raving about it, but to see it in person and how he utilizes, it is special. There are guys with speed that don't know how to use it. He knows how to use it. He uses it to get in and out of breaks, to set up defensive backs. There aren't too many guys that are fast and can play ball. But he's one of those guys. The majority of guys I've been around that have been fast are not as good. You have to learn how to control your speed. Tyreek runs different than any other human being. I'm a long-stride, power guy. But Tyreek runs with shorter strides. I've never seen anyone run like Tyreek and be fast at doing it that way. Sometimes I sit there and say, 'What the heck is that?' It's like he's some type of another being."

Hill's speed is what generates a lot of attention and it's a major reason for his big-play ability. But his other qualities—a rare ability to track deep passes and a vertical jump that allows him to high-point throws—are just as important for the 5'10" Hill to outmaneuver bigger defensive backs. "There aren't many guys out there like him," Matt Moore said. "I've played with some good ones, but he's different. To know he can track down any ball and use his speed and his talents to get open the way he does, it's a nice feeling knowing you've got him out there."

Chiefs safety Tyrann Mathieu has never played against Hill in a game—only in practice as a teammate. But after the Vikings game,

Mathieu tweeted about Hill's collection of skills. "I played with some damn good ball players," Mathieu tweeted. "[Hill] is top 5."

Mathieu later elaborated on that social media post. "Most players are competitive, but he has competitive greatness," he said. "What I mean by that is in tough situations, critical moments, only a few people can make certain plays. He's one of those players. The only way you can cover him is to have that competitive greatness yourself. You have to know the ball is coming to him and in your mind you believe you can make the play. You just have to match his energy, his attitude, and that's hard to do. He's on another level most of the time."

This is high praise from Mathieu, who has been a teammate of Odell Beckham Jr. while in college at LSU, Larry Fitzgerald while with the Arizona Cardinals, and DeAndre Hopkins while with the Texans. "Those guys can catch most balls, but I've never seen anybody do it like [Hill], being that size," Mathieu said.

Chiefs defensive coordinator Steve Spagnuolo was with the New York Giants in 2017 when he coached against Hill. He called preparing a gameplan for Hill to be a dilemma. "I don't know if I've seen anybody attacking the football better than he does, and he forces a defense to become simpler," Spagnuolo said. "Part of that is: a) because of his abilities and b) because of what Andy and Eric do with him, how much they move him around. He's always in motion. That creates some headaches. Teams that might want to play man coverage might want to think twice about that."

Hill is one of five players in NFL history with 20 or more 40-yard touchdowns at age 25 or younger. The others are Hall of Famers Bob Hayes, Randy Moss, Gale Sayers, and Lance Alworth. But it's not all just speed. Against Houston in his first game back from the injury,

Hill made a leaping 46-yard catch. NFL NextGen stats measured him with a 40.5-inch vertical jump on that reception.

Hill shrugged at the mention of most of these plays, though he did make fun of the notion that it appeared at first that Moore had thrown the ball too far on his 40-yard pass against Minnesota. "Can't nobody overthrow me," Hill said.

Cardinals defensive coordinator and former Denver Broncos head coach Vance Joseph is one who believes Hill doesn't get enough credit for his collection of all-around receiving skills. "I've seen some reports where guys are calling him the best receiver in the league, and they're not far-fetched,'" Joseph said. "This guy is explosive. He can really stop and start, which makes him a great route runner. And he catches the ball in traffic, which is really rare for little receivers. Tyreek and Antonio Brown are the two little guys who can really finish in traffic down the field, and that's a special [quality]. When you're facing a guy like him, you have to obviously challenge him. You have to challenge him and you have to have your safeties overlap to erase some of the deep balls. When you watch him on deep balls, he is really outrunning the corner and outrunning the safety. The safeties have to do a good job of having great angles to him and having enough depth to overlap his speed."

Judging purely by the stats, Hill isn't the most productive receiver in the NFL. Since the start of the 2017 season when Hill became a regular, he has 220 receptions for 3,522 yards and 26 touchdowns. Those numbers rank 16th, seventh, and third, respectively, among NFL receivers. Even his own teammate, Kelce, has more catches and yards.

Stats aren't always the best way to gauge the contributions of Hill, who is kind of in his own mold as a smaller player and is much more than a slot receiver. He became even more valuable to the Chiefs when the strong-armed Mahomes replaced Alex Smith as the starting quarterback two years ago. Hill can now be targeted almost anywhere on the field. He proved it with his long-distance catch against the Atlanta Falcons in the 2018 preseason. "Just do the math," Spagnuolo said. "You'd like to spy somebody on the quarterback and you'd like to double [Hill]. So you start adding it up, and who's left to cover all the other receivers? That's why I say defenses need to become simpler because of him."

When Mahomes became the starter, it helped expand Hill's range. He had 1,479 receiving yards in 2018. That's not only a Chiefs record, but also the most for any receiver who ever played for Reid as a head coach. "Pat is a beast," Hill said. "He helps us evolve all of our games. Not only me. It's fun. He can obviously throw it deep. I love going deep."

Reid said Hill has put in plenty of work to become one of the game's best receivers. "Instead of just the vertical game or the quick-screen game, he's worked on all the intermediate routes that take a little bit of a feel," Reid said. "How do you get that? You get that from working with your quarterback hour after hour after hour. They come out and they can time that thing up against a particular look. He's gotten a lot better in those areas. He understands what it takes to play that position. Remember he was a running back at one point in his career in college. So this was a new world for him."

Hill looked like the best player on the field against the Vikings, and the Chiefs needed him to be to secure an important victory without Mahomes. "He's definitely the most explosive person in the league," Mahomes said. "The way he's developed as a receiver over these last few years, I know he's going for that top spot. I know there are a lot of great receivers in this league, but I'm glad I have Tyreek on my team for sure."

11

SCHWARTZ SITS, BUT MAHOMES RETURNS

"Obviously, too many mistakes. I take full responsibility for the whole thing. I have to have my team ready to go. Then, I have to do a better job, as we all do as coaches and players, in the roles that we have. There are some good things within the end result. There were some positive things as we went along. But unfortunately, the negative things masked that and caused the end result, which is a loss. We have to fix that. We've got a good locker room. These are guys that work hard and practice hard and fast. We'll get back on it, but we have to learn from it, obviously."

—Andy Reid after the Kansas City Chiefs' error-filled performance against the Tennessee Titans in Week 10.

IF THERE WAS A DAY during the 2019 season when the Kansas City Chiefs' Super Bowl aspirations felt most distant, it was in Week 10 in Nashville, where the Chiefs lost 35–32 to the Tennessee Titans. Patrick Mahomes not only returned to their lineup, but also did so sensationally, throwing for 446 yards and four touchdowns. The Chiefs got a big game from Tyreek Hill, who caught 11 of Mahomes' throws for 157 yards and a touchdown. The defense allowed just two touchdowns to the Titans in the first three-and-a-half quarters.

And the Chiefs still couldn't win.

In the final six-and-a-half minutes, they allowed two touchdowns. In the final two minutes, they botched two field-goal attempts, either one of which would have at least put the game into overtime. Forget about the Super Bowl for a moment. Just winning the AFC West and getting into the playoffs looked at the moment like a formidable challenge. The Oakland Raiders beat the Los Angeles Chargers that week to raise their record to 5–4, a half-game behind the 6–4 Chiefs.

The Chiefs couldn't know it then, but their season would turn and do so dramatically after this defeat. They wouldn't lose again in the six remaining regular-season games or three in the postseason. The Chiefs would win all nine games by at least seven points and seven by double-digit margins. They would trail in the second half just one more time in the regular season, and that was for only 16 seconds—or long enough for Mecole Hardman to return a kickoff 104 yards for a touchdown in a Week 17 game against the Chargers. Their defense would at times lead the way, starting with a Week 11 game against the Chargers.

But that was impossible to see in the despair of their collapse against the Titans, which gave the Chiefs their fourth loss in the last six games. A symbol of their troubles was their offensive line. The Chiefs began the game without two injured starters, left tackle Eric Fisher and right guard Laurent Duvernay-Tardif. During the game the Chiefs lost two other starting linemen, including right tackle Mitchell Schwartz, leaving them one additional injury away from having to play backup tight end Blake Bell on the offensive line.

Schwartz missed only three snaps. His knee injury turned out not to be serious. But for the first time in his seven-and-a-half NFL seasons—the first four with the Cleveland Browns and the last three-and-a-half years with the Chiefs—Schwartz was on the sideline while his team's offense was on the field. When he left the game, Schwartz ended a streak of 7,894 consecutive snaps, the longest current streak in the league. "It's amazing. It honestly is," Mahomes said of his teammate's now-ended streak. "You could hear the guys in the huddle… wondering if he could get back out there [or] if we were going to try to call a timeout so he could get back on the field."

Schwartz began his career in 2012 and played those four seasons in Cleveland as a teammate of offensive tackle Joe Thomas, who put together a streak of more than 10,000 snaps before having to leave the Browns' lineup because of an injury. Schwartz had acknowledged how important the streak is to him. He asked to play in the final game of the 2017 season against the Denver Broncos, even though the Chiefs already had clinched the AFC West championship and were resting other key players. "We had to stop play because of me, so I had to come out there," Schwartz said after the Titans game. "Obviously, I tried to walk around a little bit after and I wasn't able to do that. I think we were in a not-so-good down and distance and I didn't want to go out there just for pride's sake, and all the sudden, my guy turns the corner and runs into Pat. Then Pat's hurt, so that's not something that I'd be stupid enough to do. It was weird. I've never done anything like that before. I knew something didn't feel right, nothing broken or anything like that. It sucks. It was seven-and-a-half years running. It's a pretty cool thing. Now I'm just normal like everybody else. It is what it is. You do inventory and make sure nothing's going in the wrong direction or drastically wrong, and I've been able to avoid that."

It's unusual for Schwartz to even miss any practice time. He sprained his ankle midway through the 2016 season, his first with the Chiefs, and sat out a couple of practice sessions. The Chiefs listed him as questionable for that week's game against the Indianapolis Colts on their final injury report of the week. But Schwartz, of course, answered the bell come gameday. "As a lineman you pride yourself on being out there at all times," Schwartz said. "There's a lot of luck involved with that. Just the nature of football—it's easy to get rolled up on and easy to get injured. I've been fortunate that hasn't happened. You always get dinged up and you have things happen, but there's never been a time where I was doubting I would be out there. Even in the middle of a game, you get your bumps and bruises, and 'Oh, that feels a little sore. I'm sure that will hurt more tomorrow than it does today.' But you just keep rolling."

There was a Thursday night game with the Browns in 2014 when his streak appeared in jeopardy. The Browns had a big lead late in the game when they sent a replacement out on the field. "We were up pretty big, and the line was on the field during a timeout," Schwartz said. "They sent [from the sideline] a lineman to the field, and everybody was just kind of wondering what's going on. He was like [to Thomas], 'Joe, you're out.' Joe was like, 'Uh, no, that's not happening.' We played that series and went back to the bench. Our line coach was like, 'Mitch, do you want to come out?' I was like, 'No, I'll stay in.' That's really been the only time it's been close."

Schwartz said he hasn't told Andy Reid or offensive line coach Andy Heck he would prefer to stay in the game no matter the situation. That's just understood because of the position he plays. "You feel the responsibility to your teammates to be out there if you can,"

Schwartz said. "Obviously, if you can't, you don't want to put the team at risk or put yourself at risk. If you're out there at a substandard level and that affects the team, you wouldn't want to see that happen. There is an element of being smart about it if a situation does arise, but as a lineman, you always feel like you really want to be out there."

Schwartz gets lost publicly in the crowd of Chiefs offensive talent, but he's been an important part of their success. They won the AFC West championship in each of his four seasons with the Chiefs in part because he's kept top pass rushers from divisional rivals like Denver's Von Miller and Melvin Ingram of the Chargers off the back of first Alex Smith and later Mahomes.

The Chiefs acquired Eric Fisher, their left tackle, with the first overall pick of the 2013 draft. "You want to make sure you're secure on the edge and at the same time give the quarterback an opportunity to step up when he needs to with a firm inside three," Reid said. "Having two tackles, particularly in this division, ends up being very important. I think [Schwartz] probably could play anywhere along the line. He's highly intelligent, not only in the books, but also football-wise. I think we could probably swing him wherever, left tackle included, if needed. [Fisher] did a good job for us, so that would be more of an injury thing than anything."

Schwartz plays on the right side, and tackles on that side of the ball have become more important as teams operate more frequently with the quarterback in shotgun formation. With the quarterback under center, left tackles are the premium position because they protect the blind side of a right-handed quarterback. But operating from the shotgun, quarterbacks are better able to see the rush coming from all angles. The Chiefs in 2019 were fifth in the NFL in number of snaps from a shotgun formation with 746.

Defenses have adjusted as well. Premier pass rushers often used to come solely from the right side of the defense, so they could attack a quarterback's blind side. But many top rushers now move around a defensive formation, and some line up on the left side of the defense. "The league is starting to realize that in general," Schwartz said. "Back in the day, there was a lot more under-center quarterback play, the quarterback taking the drop from under center, and he really can't see over to his left. Now, he starts behind the line of scrimmage. In terms of vision, he can see everything, feel everything. You have quality guys week after week. I don't think it's a position where you can just stick a guy and hope you survive anymore. You have to have a good player at both tackle spots. And I think teams are realizing now, especially, you have to have a balanced line across the board. If you have one or even two guys who are not pulling weight, then you can get exposed. So I think realizing balance is the key, and having solid or really good players at all five spots is as good as you can get."

The good news to come from the Titans game was that Mahomes showed no ill effects from his knee injury. He made his usual variety of effective throws, including a jump pass to beat the pass rush that Hardman took 63 yards for a touchdown. Mahomes had in fact been working recently on just such a throw with quarterbacks coach Mike Kafka. "That's Pat," Hardman said. "That's all you've got to say. He's Pat, so that's what he does. He maneuvers in the pocket. He makes throws that people can't make. I think he made his name known for doing stuff like that."

Mahomes came out of two games later in the season—one against the Raiders and the other against the Chicago Bears—but only in the fourth quarter after the Chiefs had safe leads. He did suffer one more injury later in the season, and that was to his passing hand against the New England Patriots, but he didn't come out of that game. "The knee is feeling fine," Mahomes said after the Titans game, "just how we expected going into the game. I trust in [the doctors and trainers], and they told me I was ready to go…I had full confidence I was going to be able to play this game."

12

THE DEFENSE RISES IN MEXICO

"I definitely feel like I could throw it pretty far. I don't know about 100 yards, but I definitely felt like I could throw it pretty far. For me I didn't feel the altitude too much. I think, for me, the biggest thing was I scrambled more than I usually do, so I was pretty tired at the end anyways. So it's definitely, we're definitely high up there. I saw guys that were getting a little tired there, but they fought through it and found a way to get a win."

—Patrick Mahomes after leading the Kansas City Chiefs with 59 rushing yards against the Los Angeles Chargers during their game in Mexico City.

WHEN THE KANSAS CITY CHIEFS held a news conference in April of 2019 to introduce new defensive end Frank Clark, who had been acquired in a trade with the Seattle Seahawks, the player who showed up first to publicly welcome him wasn't one of their longtime veterans. It was another one of their new arrivals, safety Tyrann Mathieu.

That may have been a small gesture on Mathieu's part, but it was telling nonetheless. Mathieu signed with the Chiefs in March, but before he had been able to so much as practice with the Chiefs, he was already the face of their heavily renovated defense. The Chiefs were an overtime loss to the New England Patriots in the previous season's AFC Championship Game away from reaching the Super Bowl, a failure directly traced to their faulty defense. They overhauled the defensive coaching staff and base system and acquired as many as seven new regulars to try to make quick and dramatic improvement.

Mathieu, along with Clark, were key pieces in the rebuilding effort, and he didn't waste time trying to get the turnaround started. He embraced the defensive leadership role that was vacated earlier in the offseason when the Chiefs released safety Eric Berry. They also parted with another vocal veteran, linebacker Justin Houston. "I've always been quiet for the most part, especially any time I've come into a new environment," said Mathieu, who joined the Chiefs after five seasons with the Arizona Cardinals and one with the Houston Texans. "Obviously, you'd like to have respect for the people around you. But for me it's about obviously embracing the guys around me and believing in them, but knowing that there's a certain direction we want to go in, and everybody can't lead you in that direction. So a lot of the guys on our side of the ball, we have to really follow somebody in the right direction. Hopefully, I can lead those guys in that direction."

The Chiefs weren't shy about allowing him to take that role. Indeed, they liked his leadership skills from his time with Arizona and Houston, one reason he was signed to a three-year, $42 million contract. In a loud statement about just how much the Chiefs felt they had to have Mathieu, he was the highest paid safety in league history at the time he signed his contract. "You can acquire as many great players, as many talented players as you'd like," general manager Brett Veach said when the Chiefs signed Mathieu. "But until you have a catalyst to make it go, things will never work out the way you want. [Mathieu] was the catalyst that we had to have."

Mathieu quickly became the defensive version of Patrick Mahomes, the player everyone else on his side of the ball listened to when he talked. "If you meet him, you see the mentality and the leadership that he has just by being himself," Mahomes said prior to the season. "That's a huge thing that he's going to bring to this team. He's going to come in with the mentality of: he wants to be great, he wants to be known, [he wants] the Kansas City Chiefs to be known as a great defensive team, a team that can shut people down. He brings that mentality as he walks through the locker room, and I think that's going to be something that we will utilize this year."

The Chiefs got their money's worth from Mathieu in his first season in Kansas City. Besides being their defensive leader, he excelled on the field. He was named first-team All-Pro for the second time in his career. His teammates voted him as the team's Most Valuable Player instead of such players as Mahomes or Travis Kelce. "It says a little about myself but really more about the people I'm surrounded by," Mathieu said. "A lot of those guys inspire me really as much as I inspire them. Those guys give me the confidence I need to do my job at a high level. A lot of those guys, they'll follow me anywhere. I'm trying my best to lead them in the right direction. I take great pride in it."

The Chiefs used Mathieu in a variety of roles, including in coverage on slot receivers. He led the team with four interceptions and also had two sacks. His success, and that of the defense as a whole, manifested itself in an obvious way in Week 11's 24–17 win against the Los Angeles Chargers in Mexico City. He had an interception that allowed the Chiefs to have a halftime lead. With the offense stagnant and in need of some assistance—the Chiefs had just 109 first-half yards—Mathieu delivered. His interception and 35-yard return gave the Chiefs the ball at the Chargers' 6, and Kansas City scored its only first-half touchdown from there.

The defense as a whole also delivered. They intercepted four passes, including two in the fourth quarter. The Chargers had four possessions in the final period of a game they trailed by seven points, and the Chiefs shut them out. The game marked the start of the Chiefs' defensive turnaround. In the regular season's first 10 games, the Chiefs allowed 23.9 points per contest. They yielded 11.5 points per game over the final six to lead the league during that span.

Teammates credited Mathieu for leading the turnaround. "Tyrann Mathieu, that's the Landlord right there," defensive lineman Chris Jones said after the Super Bowl. "He commands the field, and rent was due [in the Super Bowl]. Everybody had to pay their rent, and we did. He held everyone accountable since Day One."

It's not unusual for a high-dollar free agent to become a significant and immediate presence for his new team off the field as well as on it. But many such players find it takes time to find their place in the new locker room. The Chiefs' major free-agent addition the season before, Sammy Watkins, acknowledged being more of a locker room observer his first year in Kansas City.

Mathieu didn't have such reservations. He jumped right in. He sensed the Chiefs needed to change their stale defensive culture and he was right. The Chiefs were solid on defense in their early seasons under Andy Reid but not in recent seasons as longtime stars like Berry and Houston started to fade. "We're really trying to build a defense with an attitude," Mathieu said. "Anytime you can have 10, 11 guys with a chip on their shoulder, with an edge, a certain kind of presence, a certain kind of attitude, a kind of swagger, you can create a collective identity. We've got a good group, a young group. As long as me, as a leader, gets everybody to buy in, I think we'll be all right."

In addition to Mathieu and Clark, defensive end Alex Okafor, linebacker Damien Wilson, cornerback Bashaud Breeland, and safety Juan Thornhill were among the new defensive players the Chiefs acquired to improve the defense. Each wound up playing well at least in spots during the season. But the Chiefs held up Mathieu as the example for how they wanted those players and others to work. "The way he plays, the way he goes about his profession here, for young guys it's invaluable," Andy Reid said. "You bring in a veteran player that does it the right way. He's going to go out and he's going to attack it and study and take the leadership role, handle it the way you're supposed to handle it on and off the field. He's kind of fun to be around. He's [all] business. He shares that with the guys around him. He has those instincts. You can't teach that part. That's what he's had. He had it in college and he's had it in the NFL. He works hard every snap, and that's infectious. Along with Clark being Frank and going 100 miles per hour every snap, that kind of stuff is contagious."

Mathieu's teammates had responded positively at his previous stops. "When I went to Houston, I really just went there not just trying to be a leader," he said. "I was just being myself. A lot of guys, they feed off me. I'm extremely prideful in what I do. I think a lot of guys take heed of that. They look up to that. It will be my job to come in here, try to give some direction, try to give guys some motivation [and] some inspiration, and then be an everyday factor. I want to be the same guy I am in the weight room that I am on the football field. I want to…help the young guys, help my teammates, help everybody be confident, and make everybody feel like they're special."

Mathieu was the one who gathered his teammates around him for final words every week as pregame warmups ended. It was Mathieu, who later in the season took responsibility for directing his teammates' immediate attention to the next week's big game against the Patriots after a big win against the rival Oakland Raiders. "This organization was blessed to have Eric Berry…a great leader, tough, all those things," Reid said. "Before that I was with Brian Dawkins. I've been lucky to be around some really good safeties. They're all different in their own way, but they're all great football players with great instincts and good leaders. They lead a different way. This kid here, he's a special kid. He's not the biggest guy. You're not looking at one of those huge safeties, but, man, is he a good football player. He just gets it."

That's much of the reason the Chiefs paid a premium price to get Mathieu. "I truly feel like they brought me here, obviously, to make plays but to kind of set the tempo and set the energy in the building," Mathieu said. "I've always been a team guy. I feel I can go into any locker room and fit in for the most part, really relate to most of the guys in the locker room. That's all I tried to do here is come in, play my role, be a veteran, and be a leader on the defensive side, and just try my best to kind of bring the team together, and keep the team together whether things are going good or bad. The first thing with leadership is you have to understand your surroundings, your environment, and the kind of people you're dealing with day to day.

Here we had such a young team, such a vibrant team with a lot of different personalities. I've just tried to be myself."

Defensive coordinator Steve Spagnuolo called Mathieu the "glue" of the defense. "He's the guy that can get in the huddle in practice and say, 'Hey, we need to step it up,'" Spagnuolo said. "You need guys like that. That stuff I value as a coordinator. It makes my job a lot easier."

Spagnuolo relayed a conversation he had with an old friend who had coached Mathieu before the seventh-year safety signed with the Chiefs. "He said something to the effect of, 'He changed the building the minute he walked through the door,'" Spagnuolo said. "It just stuck with me as we evaluated the process. That kind of rang true. That's the kind of guy he is. He's dynamic, has a lot of energy. Guys gravitate to him. He's serious about what he's doing. When you're a coach and you have a player like that, that helps."

The team's Most Valuable Player was an inspirational voice in the locker room. "Everything that he does and everything he that he says, he speaks it into existence," Clark said. "I love hearing him speak to us on Sundays because it's a different type of motivation. He's going to bring the best out of everyone around him, whether you're a first-year guy, a fifth-year guy, a Pro Bowler, an All-Pro, Super Bowl-winning quarterback. He's a motivator. It's not just about him being on defense. He's going to motivate the whole team. I'm sure he's motivating QB1. I'm sure he's motivating the Cheetah. I'm sure he's motivating the coaches to coach better."

He's also a teacher. Mathieu had a role in the development of Thornhill, whose season ended when he tore his ACL in the final regular-season game against the Chargers. The rookie had showed a lot of promise up to that point. "He just told me to be myself," said

Thornhill, who had three interceptions in 2019 and returned one for a touchdown in the December win against the Raiders. "When you be yourself, you make more plays. I'm just going out there and having fun, and that's probably the biggest tip he's given me all year. The guy is a heck of a player. I wouldn't be where I am now if it wasn't for him. He's always giving me little, small tips that help me become a better player. He's taught me a lot."

On the field the Chiefs have asked much of Mathieu. The versatile player lined up as a slot cornerback on 411 snaps, safety 359 times, and linebacker 224 times. "He wears a lot of hats," defensive backs coach Sam Madison said. "Early in the year, we just wanted to put guys in situations to be comfortable. He understands the defense. Since he's been at LSU, he's played all over the place. It was just a natural fit for him. He's taken to it very well. I talked to him [early in the season], telling him just to be patient and try not to go out there and find the plays but let them come to him. That's what he's been doing."

Asked whether the Chiefs were ever concerned about overloading Mathieu, Madison said: "We thought about it. But when that kid comes into the meeting rooms, he has all the answers that we ask. When we threw him out there, it doesn't really seem to bother him. We knew all the different positions that he played previously and we're just trying to apply it to what we have. He wants to be out there. He loves football. When you have players like that, you try to give them as much as possible to see what sticks and what falls by the wayside. A lot of this stuff is sticking."

Mathieu was once one of the fastest players on the field. He was a top punt returner earlier in his career. After having two serious knee injuries, he said he's not the same player he used to be athletically. But he still had a big impact for a team that needed it on and off the field. "I've grown," Mathieu said. "I'm in my seventh year now, and it's bigger than me. It's about me playing well but getting other people around me to play well. One of the best decisions I made was coming here."

Mathieu's successful season, including his first Super Bowl championship, turned him into something of an icon among younger players. At least a dozen of them during media interviews at the 2020 NFL Scouting Combine in Indianapolis said they tried to model their games after Mathieu's. Clemson defensive back K'Von Wallace, who the Philadelphia Eagles drafted in the fourth round, discussed what he likes about Mathieu's game. "His versatility, instincts, his tenacity to play the game, his physicality, his brains," Wallace said. "He's always pointing at his head, talking about…how smart he is. I feel like I got a high FBI—football intelligence—and with that just the way he just plays the game with passion and love, and his teammates love him. He's a captain. He's a leader in that locker room. I definitely want to model my game after him."

These endorsements are proof of the ground Mathieu covered since arriving in the NFL. He was looked at as a risky pick in the 2013 NFL draft, which is why he lasted until the third round. LSU kicked Mathieu off the team in 2012 for multiple violations of the school's substance abuse policy for athletes. "It's humbling because I'm not perfect," Mathieu said. "I'm not the prototypical athlete. I'm not the fastest. I'm not the biggest. I'm not the strongest. I won't even grade well, right? What a lot of those guys respect is that I play for much more than myself. Every team I've been on, people have been able to see that. I play for the guy next to me more so than myself. I think a lot of young guys, they like that. Obviously, every team I've played on, everybody wants to try to act like me or emulate my attitude or energy level. It's a good feeling to have guys that are far younger than me watching me and really studying me. I feel like I'm on a bigger mission. It's not necessarily about myself. I feel like I'm inspiring a lot of people. I think football is really small. It's obviously a platform for me. I think a lot of people look up to me just because of some of the adversity I've been able to overcome."

13

DOMINATING THE AFC WEST

"That's what we've expected all season long. I think you have seen it week by week, the defense getting better. Special teams made great plays today, and then the offense, we're just playing with the flow of the game. I mean, we've been in every type of football game it seems like now. So we need to find ways to win each and every game because every game flow is different. I feel like today it was about letting the defense eat and us taking the opportunities to score when we can."

—Patrick Mahomes after the Kansas City Chiefs put together their most complete game of the season to date.

THE KANSAS CITY CHIEFS EFFECTIVELY locked up their Week 13 victory against the Oakland Raiders at Arrowhead Stadium late in the second quarter the way they always seem to against Oakland quarterback Derek Carr—with an interception. This one—returned 46 yards for a touchdown by rookie safety Juan Thornhill—gave the Chiefs a 21–0 lead in a game they would go on to win 40–9.

The win effectively locked up another AFC West championship— their fourth straight—for the 8-4 Chiefs. They would clinch the next week by beating the New England Patriots while the Raiders lost to the Tennessee Titans. The Chiefs dominated their division because they dominated their divisional opponents. Kansas City went on to beat the Denver Broncos and Los Angeles Chargers later in the season to finish 6–0 against the other AFC West teams.

They're also 27–3 for a .900 winning percentage against divisional opponents during the past five seasons. Against the Raiders they're 9–1, and that one loss came by one point. Meanwhile, the Chiefs' average margin of victory in their nine wins is 15.9 points. Against the Chargers they're 9–1, and that loss also came by one point. The Chiefs' average margin of victory was 12.3 points. The Chiefs' average margin of against the Broncos is a similar 12.2 points. They are 9–1 against Denver with the lone loss coming on a Denver touchdown in the final minute. By comparison the Chiefs are 30–20 for a .600 winning percentage in regular-season games outside the AFC West in the past five seasons.

This is all a dramatic turnaround from 2012, the Chiefs' last season before hiring Andy Reid. Then they were 0–6 in division games, and five of the six losses came by at least 10 points. Even in Reid's first two years, the Chiefs were 2–4 and 3–3 against AFC West opponents.

Things started to change on November 15, 2015 against the Broncos in Denver. The Chiefs ended a seven-game losing streak against the Broncos, winning 29–13. For added measure, they intercepted Peyton Manning four times before he was pulled from the game in what would be the future Hall of Fame quarterback's last game against the Chiefs.

Still, the relief looked at the time to be temporary. Despite that road victory, the Chiefs watched as the Broncos eventually claimed a fifth straight AFC West championship and the franchise's third Super Bowl victory. But that day's developments remain significant. The win served as a turning point for the Chiefs and the AFC West as a whole, and what's happened in the division since isn't by accident. The Chiefs haven't lost to the Broncos since 2015. Their winning streak against Denver would run to nine games with a Week 15 victory against the Broncos in 2019.

A few factors play into the Chiefs' dominance over the Broncos and the rest of the AFC West. Manning's retirement at the end of the 2015 season was one. Another is that the rest of the AFC West mostly hasn't presented a strong challenge to the Chiefs. The AFC West sent only two other teams to the playoffs—the Raiders in 2016 and the Chargers in 2018—during the last four seasons. Neither team was good enough to advance beyond the divisional round.

The biggest reason is the plan Kansas City set in motion in 2013, when Reid was hired. It took a couple of seasons for the team to see significant results, but eventually the other AFC West teams were unable to keep up. "He's built a multidimensional team, particularly on offense, to where he has so many options that maybe he didn't have when he first got there," said Louis Riddick, an ESPN analyst who once worked with Reid as a Philadelphia Eagles scout. "His area of expertise being the offense, he's built it into a juggernaut in terms of how they can play, and I think that's what's making the difference in Kansas City. It's worked perfectly. They can play so many different styles. They have quick-strike ability. They have grind-it-out running ability. They have control-the-field ability. So he can just kind of do what he needs to do in order to win a game. They're in a very good spot right now."

The Broncos in 2015 had a great defense that included the so-called "No Fly Zone" with Pro Bowl cornerbacks Chris Harris and Aqib

Talib. The Broncos also had a premier pass rusher in Von Miller who, like other top AFC West pass rushers Khalil Mack of Oakland and Melvin Ingram of the Chargers, frequently lined up on the left side. To win against Denver's secondary, the Chiefs overhauled their wide receiving group. Their top four wide receivers by 2019, including starters Tyreek Hill and Sammy Watkins, arrived since 2016. They drafted Patrick Mahomes in 2017 and installed him as the starting quarterback the next season. He is 11–1 as the starter against AFC West teams, and that lone loss came in 2018 when the Chiefs' leaky defense couldn't hold a 14-point lead midway through the fourth quarter. "The first order of business is to try to win your division, and to do that you will try to build your team with an eye toward [division rivals]," Riddick said. "[Reid] had an eye on what Denver had, especially on the defensive side of the ball."

To counter Miller, Ingram, and Mack, who has since been traded to the Chicago Bears, the Chiefs in 2016 made the wise and underrated move to sign a top right tackle in free agency, Mitchell Schwartz. He has been everything the Chiefs hoped for in bolstering their protection. "There's no doubt that knowing what the AFC West was giving [Reid] in terms of matchup problems, he needed to make sure the right tackle situation was solidified," Riddick said.

There's reason to believe the Chiefs can extend their reign over the AFC West. Many of their better players are still young enough to be in the prime of their careers. Among Mahomes, Hill, Tyrann Mathieu, Frank Clark, and Chris Jones, none is older than 28. Travis Kelce and Schwartz are the Chiefs' only difficult-to-replace players who are over 30, and as well as both played in 2019, the end doesn't look to be in sight for either one. "They're still young," Riddick said.

"Look down their lineup. These are guys you can see playing for them for the next three, four, five years. Patrick's not going anywhere… They're built for the now and for the future, which is kind of scary from a competitor's standpoint. They have the right plan in place. They have the right coach in place. They have the right coach/GM relationship in place. And they have the franchise quarterback with ridiculous weapons…As long as there's nothing unforeseeable that comes in and destroys the kind of chemistry and the kind of plan they have going, there's no reason they shouldn't be considered AFC West favorites every year for the next three or four years."

The Chiefs can look back at their 2015 breakthrough against the Broncos as the moment when it all started. The Chiefs went to Denver with a 3–5 record, making a victory against the eventual Super Bowl champions look unlikely. But their time had finally come, and beating the Broncos can't be overlooked in explaining everything that has followed. "For sure that game was big," Riddick said. "Division games always mean more, emotionally and psychologically. So when you beat a team like that that's had your number, yeah, it means a ton."

Thornhill's interception of Carr in the Week 13 win against the Raiders continued a trend. Carr is 1–9 against the Chiefs in the last five years and 0–5 at Arrowhead. He's thrown seven interceptions in those five games with three touchdown passes for a dismal passer rating of 62.7. He's not the only AFC West quarterback to struggle against the Chiefs. Philip Rivers of the Chargers in the last five years was also 1–9 against the Chiefs. With 19 interceptions and 12 touchdown passes in those 10 games, Rivers also had a feeble passer rating of 71.5. The Broncos have started six different quarterbacks against the Chiefs in the last five years, and none fared well. With

12 touchdown passes and 15 interceptions, they have a combined passer rating of 68.1.

These numbers are startling compared to the numbers of the Chiefs' pass defense outside the AFC West. In divisional games over the last five years, the Chiefs allowed 37 touchdown passes but have 47 interceptions. Opposing quarterbacks have a passer rating of 71.9 and a QBR of 33.9. Outside of the division, the Chiefs allowed 85 touchdown passes with 40 interceptions. Opposing quarterbacks have a passer rating of 89.0 and a 63.0 QBR.

In the past couple of seasons in particular, the Chiefs have become the kind of team Reid always wanted to coach: one so dynamic and versatile on offense that it can overcome any obstacle an opposing defense can reasonably present. He could never quite get there with the Eagles or in his early seasons with the Chiefs. "He really loves offensive football," said former Eagles president Joe Banner, who worked with Reid for years in Philadelphia. "He loves being able to be progressive and aggressive and innovative and he's got every tool he could possibly look for to do anything he could possibly want to do. That's got to be a lot of fun. I talk to him sometimes and watch him coach. He seems to be having a lot of fun."

The Chiefs led the NFL in scoring in 2018 and averaged about a touchdown less per game in 2019, when they finished fifth in points. But they were still dynamic on offense and made up for it by improving significantly on defense. The Chiefs allowed about a touchdown less per game in 2019 than the year before. "Look at how they can win games now in particular and how balanced they've become on offense, how multifaceted they've become on offense," Riddick said. "They can truly play the kind of football that Andy wants to play.

Normally, he would like to throw the football, get a big lead on you, and then grind you down with the running game. Then on defense that allows you to kind of play a little more one-dimensional, meaning they can just rush the passer."

The Chiefs used that formula to beat the Raiders in Week 13. But the Chiefs excelled in 2019 in coming back from what in years gone by would've been overwhelming deficits. They rallied from a double-digit deficit to win two games in the regular season. They rallied from being down at least 10 points in all three of their postseason games. They trailed by 24 points in their divisional round playoff game against the Houston Texans and by 10 points midway through the fourth quarter of the Super Bowl.

Reid tried his whole career to build a team with that kind of capability. Until the past couple of seasons, many of his best offensive teams were with the Eagles. The Chiefs in his first five seasons in Kansas City had some great moments offensively with Alex Smith at quarterback but also some slumps. Their Super Bowl-winning team was just two seasons removed from a three-game stretch, in which the Chiefs scored 36 points total. Counting the Raiders win and the playoffs, the Chiefs scored at least 40 points in a game three times in 2019 and at least 30 another seven times.

Former Minnesota Vikings head coach Brad Childress served as an assistant coach under Reid during his first five seasons in Kansas City. "It's a terrible feeling for a coach and a playcaller to look at your play card and say, 'I'm not sure what we can make work,' and that's kind of what we went through [in 2017]," Childress said. "But now I don't think there's any place on Andy's card that he can't drop his finger and say, 'We can run this and run it right now and make this work' regardless of which receivers they have in the game. That's rare. There are a lot more times when you look at those hundreds of plays on the card and say, 'Damn, what play can I call here to get us a completion?' He doesn't feel that now in the very, very least. The play may be an incompletion, but he can't be thinking it's hard to find something that's going to work."

The Chiefs' offensive might and Super Bowl championship appears to have captured the attention of their divisional rivals. In the first round of this year's draft, the Chargers drafted a quarterback, Justin Herbert of Oregon. The Raiders drafted a wide receiver, Henry Ruggs of Alabama, who ran a 4.27 40 at the NFL scouting combine and could compete in a footrace against Hill. The Broncos followed by taking a wide receiver of their own, Jerry Jeudy, Ruggs' Crimson Tide teammate. Denver in the second round tried for their version of Hill by selecting K.J. Hamler of Penn State, who might have matched Ruggs' 40 time at the combine but didn't run because of an injury.

The Chiefs countered with yet another offensive threat of their own, running back Clyde Edwards-Helaire of LSU. He's slated to share backfield time with Damien Williams, who rushed for more than 100 yards and scored two touchdowns in Super Bowl LIV. "You can't do it with just one guy in today's football, so we've got a whole lot of these guys now," Reid said. "You've got a few things you can draw from. With [Edwards-Helaire] his strengths are his ability to run the zone scheme and the gap scheme that they did at LSU. He has a unique ability to push the line of scrimmage in the run game and make his lateral cut and then accelerate up the field. I'd tell you that's kind of what separated him from the other guys. He's got a real knack for that. In the pass game…as many times as you get single coverage with linebackers on that backside, it gives you some nice matchups potentially. His ability to run routes and catch the football, I think those are all pluses."

The Chiefs noted the moves made by their division rivals, but those teams have a wide gap to bridge if they're going to catch the Chiefs. "I think teams, certainly, they have to score some points against us," general manager Brett Veach said. "Even if you have a really good defense, it's hard to stop our offense. So I think teams are certainly ready for a track meet when they play the Chiefs. It's going to be an exciting time for our division. Certainly, some great players were drafted by the Chargers, the Raiders, and the Broncos. Our division is always tough and competitive, and I think talent added to those teams will make this even more exciting for our fans."

14

REVENGE AGAINST THE PATRIOTS

"I think it's just another step in this season honestly. For us we've dealt with adversity through the middle of the season as far as injuries or losses that we didn't expect to have before the season started. But this team is building every single week. The defense is getting better, the offense is still rolling and doing good things. We're still getting better. It's part of the process. It's day by day. Obviously, we wanted to get this step, win this game, win the AFC West, but we're still going, and that's how we're going to keep rolling throughout the rest of this season into the playoffs."

—Patrick Mahomes after defeating the
New England Patriots in Week 14.

IN THE MOMENTS AFTER the previous week's win against the Oakland Raiders, the Kansas City Chiefs were already on to bigger things. The victory against Oakland was in itself a big thing. Beating the Raiders, their closest pursuers in the division, allowed the Chiefs to all but lock up a fourth straight AFC West championship. Only a Chiefs collapse over the final four games of the regular season could prevent them from claiming a division title.

But the Chiefs were already focused on the next week's game against the defending Super Bowl champion New England Patriots.

"I like our chances," Tyrann Mathieu said. "This week of practice really will be about assignment discipline and technique discipline. That's what the Patriots are going to do. They are going to run the ball. They are going to throw screens. They are going to wait for you to get out of a gap. They are going to wait for a deep safety to not be deep. It starts with me this week in practice, just getting the guys ready, setting the tempo early in the week, and letting them know that we have a big game this week."

The Chiefs beat the Patriots 23–16 for their third straight win. Coupled with that day's Raiders' loss, their 9–4 record allowed the Chiefs to clinch the AFC West and celebrate a fourth straight division title in a most unlikely place, the visitors' locker room at New England's Gillette Stadium. Calling it a celebration was a bit much. The Chiefs had their minds on a bigger prize, so things were surprisingly subdued in that locker room. Some players wore T-shirts that read "The West is Not Enough," an appropriate theme for the team's frame of mind.

Even with that and the Patriots' weakened state—New England clearly was no longer the team it has been in recent seasons—it's difficult to overstate what the victory meant to the Chiefs. "I'd be lying if I said it wasn't a big-time win," Mathieu said. "It's a great team. I think everything it stands for speaks for itself. Tom Brady, I could go on and on about him and Bill Belichick. Even when we were up 20–7, two possessions, in our minds we knew that we were going to have to win the fourth quarter playing against Tom Brady."

The Chiefs did have to hold off the Patriots. Cornerback Bashaud Breeland broke up a pass in the end zone on a fourth down late in the game to seal the victory. "Not one step in that fourth quarter that we really felt like we were going to lose this game," Breeland said. "The defense the whole time, we were confident enough knowing that we were going to continue to do what we were doing. Tom Brady, he's the GOAT. You're not just going to shut him out a whole entire game. So for us to do what we did against him, it was a glorious moment. This is the type of game that we wanted to come play to really test where we're at. We've had our ups and downs throughout the season. We felt like this was the point that really can help us get over the hump and propel us to where we want to be."

To the Chiefs and much of the rest of the NFL, the Patriots were the beasts, having represented the AFC in the previous three Super Bowls. New England was also the hill that the Chiefs died on the previous season when the Chiefs lost in the AFC Championship Game in overtime. That is why after the game against Oakland, a team the Chiefs had beaten nine times in the last 10, the Chiefs were more interested in the upcoming task. Having the Patriots next on the schedule can have that kind of effect on the team. "We have to beat them," Sammy Watkins said of the Patriots. "It's something we have to do. The path that we want to go on, the things we want to achieve this year, this is a have-to win."

Legacies have been built, for better or worse, on how players and coaches have fared against the Patriots. New York Giants quarterback Eli Manning has a .500 career record as a starter overall but is considered a Hall of Fame candidate because his team went 2–0 against the Patriots in the Super Bowl. Andy Reid has been defined, in part, by his inability to beat the Patriots in the postseason. Reid is 0–3 against Belichick and New England in the playoffs, including a loss with the Philadelphia Eagles in Super Bowl XXXIX, one in the divisional round of the 2015 season, and then the 2018 AFC title game.

Chiefs defensive coordinator Steve Spagnuolo, however, was the Giants' defensive coordinator when they beat the 18–0 Patriots in Super Bowl XLII. "If you're ever able to able to defeat a team that is run by Bill Belichick and has a quarterback like Tom Brady, you have to feel pretty good about that," Spagnuolo said. "But easier said than done. They're the elite. All of us, if we want to get to where we want to go, you have to find a way to do some good things against a team like this."

The Chiefs have built their team over the years with an eye toward beating the Patriots. They drafted and developed players like Patrick Mahomes, Tyreek Hill, and tight end Travis Kelce in an attempt to have a high-powered offense capable of keeping pace with Brady and also versatile enough to overcome the differing defensive looks the Patriots present from week to week.

During the offseason the Chiefs renovated a defense that allowed 80 points to the Patriots in two games last season—37 in the AFC Championship Game and 43 in a regular-season loss. They brought in Spagnuolo and a new defensive staff and added players like end Frank Clark and Mathieu. "I understand what the Patriots [represent]," Mathieu said the week of the game. "They represent consistency, excellence. They've always been the team to beat and they always play their best when it really matters. It will say a lot about where we are as a team. This is a good test for us going forward. They present a lot of different things. They're a gameplan team. They're going to try to target what they feel are the weaknesses in our players. If we can succeed against a team like this, a good team, a quality team, a championship team, then you realize you can do it against anybody."

The series between the Chiefs and Patriots was not one-sided since Reid arrived in Kansas City. The Chiefs, in fact, landed a couple of heavy blows that looked at the time like they might have some lasting effects on not only this rivalry, but also the balance of the AFC as well. In 2014 the Chiefs routed New England on a Monday night at Arrowhead Stadium. The game was so one-sided it looked at the moment like the Patriots dynasty and Brady's time as one of the NFL's great quarterbacks were coming to an end. The Chiefs led 17–0 at halftime and coasted to a 41–14 win. They rushed for more than 200 yards. They intercepted Brady twice and returned one for a touchdown. The Chiefs even drove Brady to the bench. He was replaced late in the game by a rookie named Jimmy Garoppolo, who played better than Brady that night. But the best quarterback in the game was the Chiefs' Alex Smith, who threw three touchdown passes. That led to Belichick's infamously curt "On to Cincinnati" line in the postgame press conference.

In 2017 the Chiefs walked into what looked like an ambush in New England. The game was the season opener, which was being played in New England to coronate the Patriots as defending Super Bowl champions. The home team had won 13 of the previous 14 night games that traditionally begin the NFL season. The Patriots jumped to an early 17–7 lead, but the Chiefs came back with three fourth-quarter touchdowns to pull away with a 42–27 win. At that point all things looked possible for the Chiefs. The Chiefs again ran with ease over the Patriots, recording almost 200 rushing yards this time. Smith was again the best quarterback on the field with 368 yards and four touchdowns. Brady completed less than half his passes, was sacked three times, and failed to throw for a touchdown.

Neither time were the Patriots or Brady dead. They recovered in 2014 to win the Super Bowl. They emerged in 2017 to reach the Super Bowl, where they lost to the Eagles coached by former Chiefs offensive coordinator Doug Pederson.

The Chiefs had those regular-season victories against New England but couldn't beat the Patriots in recent years when it counted the most. The Patriots beat the Chiefs in a 2015 playoff game 27–20, though the game wasn't as close as the score might appear. The Chiefs fell behind by 15 points in the third quarter and chased the Patriots the rest of the way. Brady was the better quarterback in this game, throwing for 300 yards and two touchdowns.

Then came the two games in 2018, when the Chiefs were no longer fringe contenders in the AFC but legitimate threats to the New England dynasty. The Chiefs showed in these games that they had closed the gap on the Patriots but still had more work to do in order to close it. In the regular season, Mahomes and the high-scoring Chiefs were held without a touchdown in the first half and trailed by 15 points. They then scored 31 second-half points on four Mahomes touchdown passes and tied the game with three minutes left. But the Chiefs couldn't prevent the Patriots from driving for the game-winning field goal as time expired. New England won 43–40.

As painful as that result was, it was the AFC Championship Game that cut to the bone. After being shut out in the first half, the Chiefs scored four touchdowns to take a 28–24 lead with two minutes left. The Chiefs appeared to effectively end the game on New England's drive when cornerback Charvarius Ward intercepted a Brady pass.

But the Patriots kept the ball because Chiefs linebacker Dee Ford had lined up well offside. They went on to get the touchdown that gave them the lead, though the Chiefs hurried into field-goal range, and Harrison Butker's kick sent the game into overtime. Both teams at that point were rolling offensively. They scored 38 points between them in the fourth quarter alone (and the Chiefs again had 31 second-half points). That made the coin flip to determine which team would get the ball in overtime a significant event, one that could determine the game's winner. The Patriots called heads, and that's how the coin fell. One of New England's captains, Matthew Slater, wasted no time in telling the referee, "We want the ball."

The Chiefs forced the Patriots into a third-and-10 play three times on their drive, but Brady and New England converted each time. The Patriots went on to score the touchdown that ended the game and at that point the Chiefs' best chance to reach the Super Bowl since 1970. Mahomes and the Chiefs never got a chance with the ball in overtime. "You have to take in the hurt," Mahomes said after the game. "You have to accept that this hurts. It's supposed to hurt. You put in work for this. You're doing everything you can to get to the Super Bowl and to win it. For this opportunity to fall short, it's going to hurt and…you have to go through that. At the same time when you look back and then you come back to look at the bigger picture, you know that you can build off of this feeling and use it as motivation to go out and find ways to win next time."

Brady was brilliant against the Chiefs in each of the 2018 games against the Chiefs, throwing for a total of almost 700 yards. The Chiefs matched him with Mahomes, but as good as he was, he still wasn't enough to help the Chiefs overtake the Patriots. In 2019 with Brady at 42 years old and in the final season of his New England contract, it looked at the time like it might be Mahomes' final chance to beat Brady, at least when he quarterbacked Patriots. "He's still playing at a high level," Mahomes said of Brady. "Unless he just doesn't want to play, which I don't see, I expect to see him for at least a couple more years. Whenever you play a guy like this, who's won all these championships, you want to go out there and give your best effort, obviously, and you want to try to find a way to win. As far as it looks, we're going to have to go there to win at some point. It's kind of been a thing where we came close last year. When Alex was here, we did get to go there and get the win. So the guys on the team know how to. It's about trying to find the best way to do it."

The 2019 regular-season game had many anxious moments for the Chiefs. The biggest was an injury to Mahomes' passing hand. It happened when he fell awkwardly after being hit. "It was hard for him to grip the ball and do the things that he needed to do," Reid said. "But he kept messing with that hand, and I could tell he wasn't gripping all that well. He never says anything, so he doesn't make a big stink out of anything."

Mahomes had X-rays on the hand the next day, and they were negative, so he didn't even miss any practice time in preparation for the next week's game against the Denver Broncos. "It doesn't feel great right now, but it's something that you play with," Mahomes said after the game. "In this sport you're going to get hurt, you're going to bang something. So for me it's about going out there and competing and relying on my teammates to help me out whenever I'm not feeling 100 percent. I just kind of hit the ground weird when I was trying to throw that ball away and got hit, threw it away, and got tackled right as I threw it away. I knew something was wrong, but I didn't know for sure. Then I tried to fire that next pass, and it didn't look too pretty, so I kind of just let the trainers look at it. They gave me the good-to-go, and so I went out there, battled, figured out ways to throw the ball across the middle, and maybe not shoot those long shots that I usually throw but enough to get them back and still score touchdowns."

Mahomes didn't have one of his best games, but he played well enough to help the Chiefs to perhaps their most important victory of the season so far. "They play the game the right way," Mahomes said. "If they're not clicking on offense or they're not clicking on defense, they're not clicking on special teams, the other unit picks them up. And so for me, when you have a team that plays the game the right way, that finds ways to win games even if they're not supposed to win them, you know that they're going to be there in the end in the playoffs. And so for us, we understand that they're still sitting at the two or three or whatever seed it is and we understand that we're going to have to come out every single week and then when we get to the playoffs we'll probably have to play them or another great team in this AFC to try to get to the Super Bowl."

The Chiefs had to scramble before the game to avoid a forfeit. Some of their game equipment had inadvertently been left on the team's charter flight from Kansas City. After dropping the Chiefs in New England, the plane moved on to New York with the missing gear. The Chiefs didn't realize the error until the morning of the game. So there were some anxious moments for the Chiefs in getting the equipment sent back to New England. The Chiefs had a group of equipment handlers hanging out by the loading dock at Gillette

Stadium waiting on the equipment arrival. One joked the episode was giving him gray hair. The missing equipment received a police escort from the Boston airport to Gillette Stadium. When it arrived at the stadium about two hours before the game, it was rushed to the Chiefs' locker room so that the team could comply with the NFL's uniform and equipment rules. Some of the handlers ran while carrying several bags of gear. "I had to warm up in some different stuff than I played in," Mahomes said. "But it was here in time for me to be able to go out to the real warm-up. They always keep extra stuff around. They took care of us and found a way to make it work, and we just kept rolling. They let us know it would be here before we went out there. We might have had to share helmets if it didn't get here."

15

KELCE MAKES HISTORY

"You understand how important these games are and, even though we kind of have the AFC West clinched now, you understand they are still important games. You want to make sure you keep pressing on and keep getting better every single week. We knew the Broncos were playing really good football coming in and so we just attacked it with the mind-set that we were going to go out day by day and keep this process moving. We had a good day today and we get to go to Chicago next week and play a good football team."
—Patrick Mahomes after facing another AFC West rival, the Denver Broncos, in Week 15 at Arrowhead Stadium.

O**N THE SURFACE OF IT**, the play was unremarkable, particularly considering the context of a long season. Travis Kelce was allowed a free release off the line of scrimmage on a first-quarter play of the Kansas City Chiefs' 23–3 victory against the Denver Broncos in Week 15, crossed the formation to the left, and found a hole in Denver's zone coverage to catch an 11-yard pass from Patrick Mahomes. The play—and in fact the whole game against the Broncos on a snowy day at Arrowhead Stadium—encapsulated much of what makes Kelce so valuable to the Chiefs. The Chiefs converted on a third and 4, allowing them to continue what would be a scoring drive and then take a two-score lead.

But the play also gave Kelce his fourth straight 1,000-yard season, something no tight end in NFL history had ever done. Kelce would go on to have his best game of the season with 11 catches for 142 yards. Eight of the catches provided the Chiefs a fresh set of downs. "It tells everybody I'm pretty fortunate enough to be on the field for four straight years," Kelce said afterward. "It's just a bunch of numbers honestly. I'm focused on winning games and trying to get to a Super Bowl with this team and this organization like I have been since I got here. With that being said, I'm very fortunate that I have been here in the Kansas City Chiefs organization under Coach Reid, under Clark Hunt, under the unbelievable coaches that have been here. Just being able to gain their trust, that's everything in terms of a team sport. With it being a team sport, the individual accolades, I like to just put them aside and focus on how I can get better for my team."

Between Kelce's reality dating series that ran for several episodes earlier in his career to the fun-loving antics like those at the Chiefs' post-Super Bowl rally in Kansas City, it's easy to get an image of Kelce as being something less than serious about football. He fuels that images with answers like this when he's asked why he's so good at running with the ball after a catch. "I think it's just the Kansas City barbecue seeping through my pores," Kelce said. "It makes me a little slippery when I'm out there."

The truth is that behind the scenes Kelce works at football as much as any of his teammates. He's a master technician and, as a quarterback for a time in college, he understands the game. "Kelce is an expert at working in space and getting himself open in normal conditions,"

Andy Reid said after the Broncos game. "I saw it in warm-ups, and really the field conditions, I feel, didn't bother him. He was able to get in and out of his cuts. He's a great balance guy. You add that with his ability to work in space how he does, and the quarterback trusts him. You have to add that relationship, and those guys have that."

Kelce had big numbers for the Chiefs in 2019 with 97 catches for 1,229 yards and five touchdowns. They didn't match his bigger stats from the season before, but still a case could be made that Kelce was more valuable to his team than ever. The Chiefs lost Mahomes, Tyreek Hill, Sammy Watkins, and Damien Williams for at least two games apiece and had to start five different offensive line combinations because of injuries. The one constant was Kelce, who also had four touchdown catches in the playoffs—none bigger than the one in the fourth quarter of Super Bowl LIV that closed the Chiefs' deficit to 20–17. "The biggest thing with Kelce is he has an innate ability to see all 22 on the field," tight ends coach Tom Melvin said. "He understands what we're supposed to do and what they're supposed to do. His understanding of that is something that is not taught. He's got it. That's what he's got. My biggest job is preparing for what you should see, what we're doing, how to approach it, and he takes it from there. We reevaluate during practice, during games, and going in at halftime those kinds of things. The innate part of that, I marvel at that."

Backup quarterback Matt Moore didn't join the Chiefs until shortly before the regular season started and was thrust into the lineup for the injured Mahomes in a Week Seven game against the Broncos without much practice time. The first passes he threw to many of the receivers, Kelce included, came in his first game—not in practice. "He was a huge security blanket," Moore said. "Knowing there was a guy like that you could look for in a time of need and kind of ditch the ball to him, that was great to have. I haven't seen another tight end do the things he can do. It's pretty impressive. He sees things as a quarterback would. He sees things open up before they do. Then you combine that with his body control and his ability to get open, and there's not many guys like him. Really, at the end of the day, he always finds a way to create a throwing lane for you. He uses his body and his route running to get into those positions to give you a throw."

Kelce may have the record for most consecutive 1,000-yard seasons for a tight end, but calling him a tight end is a little bit of a stretch. He had more catches during the regular season lined up as a wide-out (38) or slot receiver (35) than he did as a tight end (24). "He's a special player," Reid said. "We can move him all over the place. He's got a good feel for it."

That's frustrating for opponents, including Oakland Raiders coach Jon Gruden. Kelce had 12 catches for 197 yards and a touchdown in two games against the Raiders in 2019. "You don't know where Kelce is going to be or what route he's going to run," Gruden said. "Most guys have a route tree. They run a shallow cross, a deep cross, a corner route, a middle read. Kelce is running every route that a slot receiver or a big-time wide receiver runs. They're asking Kelce to do some things that are very, very difficult, and he pulls it off. It's maddening to not only our team, but, I think, any team that plays the Chiefs."

The snowy playing conditions against the Broncos didn't bother him. "You realize it in pregame and you attack it," Kelce said. "You can't let weather get into the game or disrupt how you're playing the game. You have to go out there and be accountable for the guys next to you. That's the biggest thing in terms of mind-set: not letting anything, the other team, the weather, or whatever may be a distraction outside of the office or at home or something like that. When you go out there, you're playing for the guys next to you."

The other standout feature from the Week 15 victory was the Chiefs' defense, which held the Broncos to a field goal. Rookie quarterback and Kansas City native Drew Lock had brought the struggling Denver offense to life the week before by throwing three touchdown passes as the Broncos scored a season-high 38 points against the Houston Texans. But the Chiefs intercepted Lock once and sacked him three times. The defense still wasn't getting as much attention as Mahomes and the Chiefs' high-scoring offense but was suddenly carrying its share of the burden.

In their Week 11 game against the Los Angeles Chargers, the Chiefs had two fourth-quarter interceptions to preserve a seven-point victory. In the ensuing game, the Chiefs had an interception on Oakland's opening drive to set up a touchdown and later returned an interception for a touchdown. The next week against the New England Patriots, cornerback Bashaud Breeland had an interception that led to a touchdown and later broke up a fourth-down pass in the end zone in the final moments that allowed the Chiefs to escape with a seven-point victory. And then the defense limited the Broncos to three points. "This game means a lot honestly," rookie safety Juan Thornhill said after the Broncos game. "Guys are just coming together. When you come together, you're going to play a lot better because you know what the guy next to you is doing. That's going to allow you to play way faster. Guys are focusing more on their job instead of trying to make other plays that's not theirs. When you focus on your job and everyone does their job, you make plays."

Tyrann Mathieu had helped mentor his fellow safety. "The system isn't new anymore. We're in December," Mathieu said. "Everybody's got a good feel for what they need to do, what they can do, and what they can't do. We've got a long way to go, but I like what we're putting on tape. From this point going forward, I think it's important to play defense. I think every team that makes the playoffs, it's going to be about what their defense can do.'"

It was making for a different world for the Chiefs without the pressure of having to score in big numbers in order to win every week. "We've been kind of known these last few years of scoring all these points and putting up all these numbers," Mahomes said. "But when your defense is playing like that and they're getting the ball back to you, it's about not trying to turn the ball over and about scoring points whenever you get the opportunity to."

The Chiefs were deprived of a championship in 2018 because their defense couldn't stand up in tough times. They lost twice to the Patriots—once in the AFC Championship Game—on the last play of the game. They scored 51 points in a game against the Los Angeles Rams but still lost. They allowed 14 and 15 points, respectively, in the fourth quarter in losses to the Seattle Seahawks and Chargers. "The defense, I think, is one of the big stories of the season," Chiefs chairman Clark Hunt said. "At the beginning of the year, we knew it was going to take a fair amount of the season for that group to really come together. We had a new coaching staff, we had new players, we had a new scheme. We struggled a little bit early with that, but over the last four or five weeks, I think the defense has really stepped up."

Reid wouldn't declare that the Chiefs had arrived on defense but couldn't deny the progress. "I can tell you every week we've gotten better," he said. "We had a little bit of a hiccup at Tennessee, but other than that, it's been consistent progress forward. The players have bought in. They're flying around, making plays."

The defense early in the season looked much the same as it did last season. The Chiefs couldn't get crucial fourth-quarter stops in all four of their losses earlier in the season. Suddenly, that felt long ago. "It comes with the trials and tribulations," Frank Clark said. "You're seeing the results of all the stuff we had to go through back then: the losing, the failure, us not being able to close out a game."

16

PRIME-TIME MAHOMES

"Spags is a heck of a coach, and so you know his production from the past job. I've gotten a long-term relationship here with the guy, so I've known him for quite a few years and understand the scheme that he has, and it's a pretty solid scheme. So it's just a matter of the players buying into it and then him being able to add to it every week. And that's a compliment to both Spags, his coaches, and the players for trusting in it. They didn't start off great, but he was able to keep adding here and there because of the guys' work ethic, ability to study, and learn."

—Andy Reid on Steve Spagnuolo and the defense, which allowed just a field goal in Week 16 for the second straight week.

THE KANSAS CITY CHIEFS DESERVE every bit of credit they are given for maneuvering in the 2017 draft. They saw Patrick Mahomes' potential and then worked to get into position to select him. They didn't have to tank to draft Mahomes. They in fact had won their division in 2016.

They outsmarted the other teams. They entered that draft with the 27th pick but accurately read the draft and knew exactly where they would have to go—10th overall—to get Mahomes. Fortune has favored the bold.

But there was an element of luck involved, and they came face to face with that part of it in their Week 16 Sunday night game against the Bears in Chicago. The Bears needed a quarterback in that 2017 draft. And after trading up to the No. 2 spot, they had their pick of any, including Mahomes and Clemson's Deshaun Watson. They instead went for North Carolina's Mitchell Trubisky, a decision that was proving devastating to the Bears, who finished in third place in their division in 2019. Mahomes was still available to the Chiefs after they traded with the Buffalo Bills for the 10th selection.

Mahomes found it necessary to remind a national television audience of the Bears' decision. He was caught on camera counting to 10 on his fingers after throwing a second-quarter touchdown pass to Travis Kelce. It was an interesting move by Mahomes, who had never given the smallest of hints that he felt slighted by lasting until the 10th pick or being the second quarterback selected. It was a side of Mahomes rarely seen in public. He is a competitor to the bone—but not the kind to scold an opponent for picking the wrong quarterback.

But obviously he did feel snubbed, busting out such a gesture against this particular opponent and this particular starting quarterback. The quarterback, though, was a bit evasive when asked about it. "I don't know if there was necessarily a meaning," Mahomes said. "I was just kind of in the moment and just enjoying it. I knew it was a big moment in the game, and you look to take advantage of it when you get that opportunity against that defense. I was just out there having fun. We had a big score before the half, and I was just trying to enjoy it. You've seen me play. I play with emotion. I like to just go out there and have fun with my teammates. I think anyone that goes about it as a competitor wants to be the first guy, but you know that there's a process to it, and not everyone can be picked first. I ended up in a great situation in Kansas City, a situation where I wanted to be at, an organization that's taken me and made me the best player I can be at this time."

The move even caught some of his teammates by surprise. Running back Damien Williams understood the significance. He offered Mahomes congratulations as the quarterback was heading off the field and doing his count. "I did see him doing that," Williams said. "At first I'm like, 'What are you doing?' He didn't say [anything]. He was just counting on his hands."

Doing a celebration of his own after scoring the touchdown, Kelce didn't see Mahomes' gesture. "I can't really see Pat doing that," Kelce said. "He's a humble guy. You know what drives everyone sometimes is something deeper. I'm sure he's happy where he is, but that probably helped him in his early years, kind of gave him some motivation and gave him some fire. I think he's the type of competitor that he feels every single game, every single time he touches the football he's trying to prove something, well, not necessarily prove something but be the best he can and show the world that you know that he is the best."

Mahomes was the clear winner in the quarterback battle with Trubisky. He completed 23-of-33 passes for 251 yards and two touchdowns and also ran for a score in the 26–3, Week 16 victory while Trubisky completed 18-of-34 passes for 157 yards. "He's a good guy, a great guy who works extremely hard, and so I respect him and his game, and we see each other sometimes in the offseason, and I'm sure to catch up with him then," Mahomes said of his Bears counterpart. "I don't know if there's necessarily a rivalry. Any quarterback you play with in this league, you want to go out there and win, of course. It's not a rivalry I would say, but it is competitive, and you want to go out there and be the best any time you step out on the field."

The play that ignited Mahomes and the Chiefs against Trubisky and the Bears was a Mahomes specialty. On their first drive of the game, the Chiefs faced a third and 18, which in the NFL is often the cue to get the punt or field-goal team ready for fourth down. League-wide teams converted less than 10 percent of the time in such situations. To Mahomes and the Chiefs, those plays were a stepping-stone to better things. Mahomes was 10-of-11 on third and 18 or longer with five first downs and three touchdowns. He averaged almost 21 yards on those 11 attempts and had a perfect passer rating of 158.3.

On the third and 18 against the Bears, the Chiefs picked a play that had mirror routes on each side, and Tyreek Hill lined up from the slot on the left. Mahomes had to slide in the pocket to avoid pressure. When he let go of the ball, Hill was about four yards from the top of his route. But by the time he turned around, the ball was there for Hill to make a 19-yard gain. "That throw made me say, 'Wow!'" Rich Gannon, the former Chiefs quarterback and current game analyst for CBS, said. "I watch a lot of throws. And when I look at a throw and go 'wow,' that's a pretty significant throw because I don't do 'wow' a lot. I've seen it and I've made some throws myself, so it takes a lot."

It helps that Mahomes has options. Nicknamed the Legion of Zoom, Hill, Mecole Hardman, and Sammy Watkins are three of the fastest wide receivers in the league. Kelce is fast for a 260-pound player. Then there's the strong-armed Mahomes, who is fearless yet forces few throws. On one of his third-and-long touchdowns—a third and 18 in Week Five against the Indianapolis Colts—Mahomes was flushed by pressure to his right and threw on the run for 27 yards to Byron Pringle. The play prompted Al Michaels, calling the *Sunday Night Football* game for NBC, to shout, "Only Mahomes!"

The third-and-long completion to Hill occurred during another Sunday prime-time game. "We believe Pat can get us out of every situation," Watkins said. "I honestly think we can get a third and 30 when it comes down to it. That's how we operate. We have so many plays for every situation. It's hard for the defense to have everything down. Then we have so many guys. It's kind of a situation where people have to pick their poison."

There was more to the Chiefs' third-and-long success. They don't thrive on those plays by accident. They spend time working on those situations in practice. "We have times in training camp where it's just third and long, where we're third and 11-plus," Mahomes said. "And we're working against a defense, knowing they're more in the prime position they want to be in to try to get stops."

The Chiefs also went into each game with options they like for third-and-long situations based on the particular opponent. "There's a lot in the playbook every week for third and long," Hill said.

Mahomes has a lot of trust in the Chiefs' receivers to be where they're supposed to be on a given route. The throw in Chicago to Hill is an example. Mahomes wouldn't throw to Hill several yards short of his break if the two hadn't worked on the route during practice. The result is the completion to Hill against the Bears, a 42-yard touchdown to Hardman on third and 20 in September against the Oakland Raiders, a 46-yard touchdown to Hill on third and 21 in Week Six against the Houston Texans, and other big plays that might be warm-up-the-special-teams circumstances for other teams. The best example occurred with the season on the line. In the fourth quarter of the Super Bowl, Mahomes threw for 44 yards to Hill on third and 15 to allow the Chiefs continue what would be a touchdown drive that cut their deficit to 20–17. "Everybody may think we like being in those situations, but we don't like being in those situations," offensive coordinator Eric Bieniemy said. "We'd rather play ahead of the chains on first and second down and not put ourselves in that predicament because when it's third and whatever, now we've got to find a way to make a play."

But frequently they do, and it came to a point where the Chiefs were confident they could convert in those situations all the time. "As long as you're out there on the field and you have Pat Mahomes on your side, you've got a chance," Kelce said. "That's the key right there."

The Bears game was the second straight touchdown shutout for the Chiefs defensively. They allowed only a field goal in the previous week's game against the Denver Broncos. That continued quite a run for the Chiefs on defense. Starting with the Week 11 game, in which the Los Angeles Chargers scored their final touchdown in the third quarter and continuing until the Week 17 game against the Chargers, in which they scored their first touchdown in the second quarter, the Chiefs went a stretch of 18 quarters and allowed just three touchdowns in that span. One came in the final minute of the Week 13 game against the Raiders, and the Chiefs were ahead 38–3 at that point. Another was a trick play by the New England Patriots on a flea-flicker that took the Chiefs by surprise. The other New England touchdown came on a short field when the Patriots had blocked a punt and recovered at the Kansas City 19.

The Chiefs had become a difficult team to score against. That prospect seemed most unlikely earlier in the season when the Chiefs failed to make important fourth-quarter stops in all four of their losses. The defense that Steve Spagnuolo was brought in to fix hadn't shown much improvement from the previous year. With an offense as explosive as the Chiefs had, the defense was once again threatening to ruin a good thing.

The Chiefs anticipated some tough times early in the season when they were trying to mesh many new elements while changing from a 3-4 to a 4-3 defense. Spagnuolo resisted the temptation to veer away from his plan and stuck to it. The results over the final six regular-season games were his reward. The Chiefs had the NFL's best scoring defense over the stretch, allowing 11.5 points per game. That was a strong response to some early-season doubt about where the Chiefs might be headed on defense. "There's always a little bit of that when we struggle in anything in life," Spagnuolo said. "It could be anything, life, whatever but certainly in football. What I have learned—because there have been a couple of times when we've felt this way—I've always found it best to believe and trust in what you're doing. If you didn't believe in it and trust in it, you shouldn't have been doing it in the first place. We talked a lot about trust. We started talking about 'trust our way to improvement,' which is the way we put it, the way the coaches fed it to the guys. To the guys' credit, they embraced it."

Between a new defensive coaching staff, a new base system, and a lot of new players, the 60-year-old Spagnuolo, had much to accomplish in a short amount of time after joining the Chiefs. But he never flinched. "He's done a phenomenal job of teaching his defense in a short period of time and then getting the results from that," Andy

Reid said. "He's got the guys believing in that system. That's hard to do when you switch over."

Spagnuolo was a natural selection for Reid to replace former defensive coordinator Bob Sutton, who was fired after six seasons with the Chiefs. Spagnuolo was an assistant for Reid for eight seasons with the Philadelphia Eagles. Since then Spagnuolo had some good times and some bad. He was the defensive coordinator for the Super Bowl-winning New York Giants in 2007. But he failed in a three-season stint as head coach of the St. Louis Rams with a 10–38 record from 2009 to 2011. Then his defenses were among the worst in the league during a season with the New Orleans Saints (2012) and a subsequent stint with the Giants (2015–17).

He took a season off from coaching in 2018, a first since his career began in 1981 as a graduate assistant at the University of Massachusetts. He traveled to practice sessions around the league, including those of the Chiefs, in search of new ideas. "I'm glad I did it," he said. "I found it to be challenging and rewarding. The challenge was missing football, missing the camaraderie of coaches and players, not being at training camp. The rewards were to sit back, see a big picture view of the NFL and the game of football as opposed to being in these buildings during the season and having the blinders on of just the team you're going to play...I have oodles of notes."

Spagnuolo and Reid hired a defensive coaching staff of Brendan Daly (defensive line), Matt House (linebackers), and David Merritt and Sam Madison (secondary). All had either coached or played for Spagnuolo. "It tells you something about Spags with the people that came here with him, that we were able to recruit here," Reid said. "These are guys that he's worked with before and they have enough trust in him to come here. That tells the players that maybe this is a pretty good thing right here."

Having a defensive staff that understood Spagnuolo's system and how he worked helped speed the transition. Changing so much about the defense was still an ambitious project. The Chiefs invested heavily in their defense by signing free agents like Tyrann Mathieu and defensive end Alex Okafor, trading for Frank Clark, and drafting safety Juan Thornhill. All had an impact this season, but none was bigger than Mathieu, who played well and was a locker-room leader. "Me and Spags, I think we feed off of each other," Mathieu said. "I feel like I'm an extension of him on the football field, just trying to understand really what he wants to get done, how he sees us playing the gameplan, and for me just being the middle man, trying to relate that to our guys so they can understand. We understand when he speaks it's coming from a great place. He's a Christian man. He has strong values. On top of that, he's a pretty good football coach. One of the things I pick up on with anybody standing in front of the room is, 'Can they command the room? Can he coach every position in the room?' I think Spags can do all of that."

Spagnuolo was more hands-on than most coordinators on the practice field. At one time or another, he pulled most if not all defensive players aside for one-on-one instruction. "Sometimes it's about tackling, sometimes it's about ball awareness," linebacker Damien Wilson said after the Bears game. "It can be about anything."

Spagnuolo hammered away in defensive meetings early in the season for the players to keep believing even as things weren't going well. They listened to him in part because of what he accomplished before joining the Chiefs. "He's been where we all want to go," Wilson said of the Super Bowl. "That gives him some credibility with the guys. He kept saying it was like we were digging a well. If we stopped in the middle, we were never going to get to the water. So we kept digging. It seems to be working."

17

FITZMAGIC TIME

"It's my first time getting a bye week. I'm going to go enjoy it. It feels pretty good knowing that you had some help out there with Miami. Fitzpatrick did a pretty good job of closing that game out to help us out. We did our job out here by getting the win and closing out the division. We want more. That's the goal. We have a first week bye, but we have to stay focused."

—Frank Clark after a dramatic finish to the regular season that saw the Kansas City Chiefs defeat the Los Angeles Chargers and quarterback Ryan Fitzpatrick and the Miami Dolphins providing some help in their game against the New England Patriots.

WHEN THE MORNING OF THEIR Week 17 game against the Los Angeles Chargers dawned, the 11–4 Kansas City Chiefs were facing the likelihood of having to play again the next week in the wild-card round of the playoffs. To instead get the AFC's No. 2 playoff seed and a first-round postseason bye, they would have to beat Philip Rivers and the Chargers at Arrowhead Stadium and they had to like their chances of that. Including their Week 11 victory in Mexico City, the Chiefs had beaten the Chargers 10 times in the last 11 tries.

The Chiefs also needed another development, which seemed far more remote. They needed the 12–3 New England Patriots to lose at home to the Miami Dolphins. Those two results together would allow the Chiefs to avoid a wild-card game because the Chiefs had the tiebreaker due to their victory against the Patriots a few weeks earlier. It seemed ridiculous to seriously consider the possibility of New England losing to Miami. The Patriots had beaten the Dolphins, a team many thought was tanking for a better draft position, 10 straight seasons in New England and had also destroyed them in Miami earlier in the year.

The Chiefs, though, had no choice but to take their game against the Chargers seriously. They had too much to gain from the possibility—no matter how slim the odds. So despite having clinched the AFC West and a playoff spot, the Chiefs pushed to beat the Chargers as if the game itself was a postseason contest.

The two games started at the same time and half a country apart. On their sideline Chiefs players were unaware of how the Patriots and Dolphins were faring. The Chiefs banned the score of the Patriots game from being shown on any of the Arrowhead Stadium videoboards in case their players would lose some motivation if the Patriots built a sizable lead. But fans in Kansas City spontaneously cheered enough times during breaks in the action of the game in front of them that the Chiefs knew that the Dolphins were at least making things interesting. "I found out with the crowd," Andy Reid said. "When they hollered, I figured something good happened because it wasn't happening with us right at that moment."

Patrick Mahomes said at one point he saw Tom Brady's stats in a fantasy update on a videoboard and tried to use them to figure out whether that meant the Patriots were winning or losing. "I saw that

Brady had one touchdown and one interception," Mahomes said. "I was trying to add that together and try to see what the score was."

The games came to their conclusions at about the same time. Damien Williams scored a touchdown in Kansas City with 2:37 remaining to give the Chiefs an insurmountable 10-point lead. In New England veteran quarterback Ryan Fitzpatrick threw a touchdown pass with 24 seconds left to put the Dolphins in front of the Patriots. That touchdown scored 1,400 miles away drew one of the biggest cheers of the day at Arrowhead. It also touched off a celebration in the locker room of the Chiefs. "Obviously playing in [New England], it would be hard for them to get a win, but that's FitzMagic, man," Mahomes said. "He does things that are awesome to watch, and they found a way to get a win."

Reid was equally appreciate of Fitzpatrick's efforts. "I want to send [Fitzpatrick] some Kansas City steaks," Reid said. "He did a nice job. I can't do that though because that's tampering, so I'm not going to do that. But he deserves them. The extra week off is great to have this year. You work hard for that. Being 12–4 is a great accomplishment for our football team, and then you're rewarded with this here. I'm proud of the guys for pushing through today because that's a tough thing to do. It's not easy because you don't know the scores and you have to have the mind-set coming into this thing. I mean, the Dolphins were a 16-point underdog going into this or whatever it was. It's a great example of why you play. If you're on that field, you go 100 miles per hour and you play your heart out. Hail to the Dolphins!"

The Chiefs were clearly energized then by getting the bye, and looking back now, it's hard to overstate how the developments of the final day of the regular season benefitted them. The point could be debated whether they would have reached the Super Bowl even if New England had beaten Miami. What's fact is their path to Super Bowl LIV was far easier as the No. 2 seed than it would have been as No. 3. As the No. 3 seed, they would have played a wild-card round playoff game against a tough Tennessee Titans squad, which ended up reaching the AFC Championship Game, at Arrowhead. They would have played at New England in the divisional round and most likely at the No. 1 seed Baltimore Ravens in the AFC Championship Game. As it was, the Chiefs never had to leave the comforts of home in beating the fourth-seed (Houston Texans) and sixth-seed (Titans) on their way to the Super Bowl. Mahomes was accurate when after the Chargers game he said, "It's basically like winning a playoff game."

The bye week would have benefitted any team, but it seems to have more benefits for a team coached by Reid. His teams have gone 18–3 in the regular season after having a week off. "He does a good job of letting us heal our bodies but at the same time keeping us in that same rhythm and that same thing that we have going all season long," Mahomes said. "He has a good feel for it, understands how to make sure our heads are still in it, and we're still preparing for the next game even if we don't know necessarily who we're playing. At the same time, we're healing our bodies and making sure that we're able to play fast when we get there. That's something that he's really mastered as he's gotten his coaching experience throughout the years.

"Just staying focused is the biggest thing. Obviously, Coach Reid does a good job of preparing us by giving us the right amount of time off but at the same time keeping us in the building and keeping us preparing for whoever we get to play. I think the biggest thing about this week is making sure you're fundamentally at the right point. As seasons go on, you start losing some fundamentals there at the end. So, we kind of go back, look at ourselves and the fundamentals and prepare ourselves, so that whoever we get to play we're ready."

During the regular season bye, Reid doesn't typically have his team practice. He believes the time off is more beneficial both physically and mentally. In this particular bye week, the Chiefs practiced on Thursday and Friday in pads, emphasizing, as Mahomes said, fundamentals like blocking and tackling. "I don't know if there's a secret to that," Reid said of his post-bye week success. "If there is, I can't give it to you. I don't know what that is. I've always given players time off to get themselves back. Rest, relax, and take care of any business you need to take care of and come back ready to go for whatever is left of the season. Now the league has made part of that mandatory. The new CBA that the league has given the players [has] an extended time where the coaches have to let them go. But I was doing that quite a little bit before then. I've done it this way for a long time, and it's been fairly successful. I've had success with it. Sometimes I think it's good to step away, whether you're doing well or not doing well. Coming off a win or a loss, I think sometimes it's good to get away and get recharged."

Reid and his staff began preparing gameplans for all three of the Chiefs' possible opponents for their divisional round game: the Patriots, Texans, and Buffalo Bills. The Chiefs had already played against two of those teams, but Buffalo wasn't on their schedule. Then the coaches settled in to watch a weekend of games on TV when they initially believed they might be working. "You take what you can off of the games, knowing that you're going to get it right after that and be able to analyze it," Reid said. "At the same time, you are in the process of working and going through all of their seasons."

Though the Chiefs were the No. 2 playoff seed behind Baltimore as opposed to being No. 1 in 2018, they carried the burden of heavier expectations going into the postseason. The 2018 season was a joyride for the Chiefs, a celebration of not only the present, but also what the future for them could be as Mahomes revealed his considerable talents and potential to the organization, its fans, and the larger football world. The Chiefs thought they had a chance to accomplish big things in 2018, but seeing it happen in such spectacular fashion was eye-opening.

The 2018 Chiefs in the divisional round won a playoff game at home for the first time in 25 years, breaking a six-game losing streak. That in and of itself was a major breakthrough for a team used to January heartache. That disappointment would come the following week in the AFC Championship Game against New England, but that was more due to the way the game played out rather than the fact the Chiefs had fallen short of the Super Bowl for the 50th straight season.

So after the Chiefs rebuilt their defense and spent large sums to acquire Tyrann Mathieu and Frank Clark, the expectations for the Chiefs and Mahomes in his Year Two as the starting quarterback were real and more than those for even the Ravens, who had a 2019 season similar to that of the Chiefs the year before. "For me I think the only thing that is really different is having the experience of being able to play in games like this at Arrowhead and being able to win one and lose one," Mahomes said. "I understand that every single play counts, how much every single rep in practice counts, and how you have to take advantage of every single opportunity that you get.

You can feel it in pregame warmups. You can feel the intensity and how much faster everyone is moving around and how much every play counts. You get out there in warmups and you feel that energy and you have to make sure you maintain and can find a way to do whatever it is to put your team in a better situation every single play."

By week's end the Chiefs learned they would face Houston, which beat the Chiefs 31–24 in Week Six at Arrowhead, in their first playoff game. So Mahomes and Deshaun Watson would have a rematch. "Every team, I think, changes throughout the season," Reid said. "They develop their personality. We've all got the highs and the lows. You kind of work through that and here you sit. We're not the same as we were in the beginning. They're not the same as they were at the beginning. So here we go."

Houston rallied from 16 points down to beat the Bills and advance to play against the Chiefs. They were also down 17–3 against the Chiefs earlier in the season before coming back to win. Those would be ironic numbers given how the Chiefs-Texans game would play out. "If you've watched Deshaun Watson since college and I'm sure even since high school, they're never out of a game," Mahomes said. "He's someone that can make big plays happen no matter what the scenario is. He's going to fight until the end. You know that going into the game and you know that coming in as an offense and as a defense and as a team that you have to make sure you're on top of it all game long. It's going to be a 60-minute fight or even longer, whatever it takes. You have to make sure you come in with that mentality that you're going to play your best football every single snap."

Reid said: "They're a good football team. They don't give up. That's the way you prepare yourself. You're getting a team that's going to play to the end, play four quarters of football. We take a lot of pride in doing that. They take a lot of pride in doing it. That's what will make it a great game."

The Chiefs-Texans game would represent the latest and most important chapter in the Mahomes-Watson rivalry. The two players will always be linked. They both arrived to the NFL in the 2017 draft. After trading up in the draft, the Chiefs could have had either player. Watson went to the Texans two picks after the Chiefs drafted Mahomes.

When the two were rookies, Watson showed the Chiefs up close what they passed over in that draft. With Mahomes on the bench serving as a backup to Alex Smith, Watson threw five touchdown passes in a Sunday night game against the Chiefs, though Kansas City won 42–34.

Watson won the first head-to-head matchup against Mahomes earlier in the 2019 season when the Texans beat the Chiefs. "We actually brought [Watson] up here too before the draft and had a nice visit with him," Reid said. "I have a ton of respect for him. He's a great player. He was great in college and he's great now. He's going to do nothing but get better as he goes on, which is phenomenal for the NFL. We look forward to the challenge and the opportunity to play against him. How great is that for that National Football League first of all, having these good, young quarterbacks?"

The Chiefs would play against the Texans without one of their top defensive players, Chris Jones, who injured his calf during practice the week of the game. The Chiefs also didn't have Jones available during their loss to the Texans earlier in the season. "You aren't going to be feeling the best," Mahomes said. "You aren't going to be in your perfect, tip-top shape, but you have to have that mentality that every single day you're going to try to be great. I feel like with this team with Tyrann and with Frank and the offensive guys like Travis and Tyreek, we've built this mentality that every single day we're going to go out there and be the best players we can be."

The Chiefs had plenty of reason to feel this game against the Texans would have a different result than the first. They had a six-game winning streak, a week off, and a healthy quarterback. "We are the hottest team," Tyreek Hill said. "We have the most swag in the AFC. I know the Ravens got Lamar. The Patriots have Tom. But we've got Patrick Mahomes, baby."

18

A COMEBACK FOR THE AGES

"Obviously, we would love it. It has Lamar Hunt's name on it. We'd love to have that. At the same time, we have to go through the process and focus and we're playing a good football team. We need to go back and make a solid gameplan and then come out and play well. That's really what it is. Then good things happen."

—Andy Reid on the chance to play for the Lamar Hunt Trophy, which goes to the winner of the AFC Championship Game.

ALMOST AS SOON AS THEY had started the playoffs, the Kansas City Chiefs could see the end, and given the way they were playing, it was coming quickly. Between a blown coverage, blocked punt, fumbled punt return, and dropped passes, they were on their way to getting ousted quickly from the postseason. They trailed the Houston Texans 24–0 early in the second quarter of their divisional round playoff game at Arrowhead Stadium.

Even then, there was an odd sense of calm along their sideline, a feel of "we've got this." A team can have that sense during such times when it has someone as resourceful as Patrick Mahomes at quarterback. "Thank God we've got Pat Mahomes," Frank Clark said after the Chiefs had rallied for the 51–31 victory. "We've got an MVP quarterback back there, so there's not too much pressure on you."

This Chiefs' rally was one for the ages. After falling behind by 24 points, the Chiefs scored a touchdown on their next seven possessions and kicked a field goal on the eighth to claim the NFL's first postseason victory where a team that trailed by at least 20 points wound up winning by at least 20.

Mahomes, who finished the game with 321 passing yards and five touchdowns, never got rattled, and his teammates picked up on that cue. He gathered his offensive teammates around him when things looked their darkest against the Texans and prepared them for what was to come. "You have to talk about the year that Patrick Mahomes had, and statistically it was not like last year," Chiefs chairman Clark Hunt said. "A lot of people would say he had an even better season despite being hurt for part of it. I think a big part of him being better this year was his leadership qualities. For a 23-year-old kid last year, he was amazing as a leader, but you really saw him mature this year as a leader. You could see the entire team looking to him when times were darkest. I will go back to the beginning of the second quarter. Patrick was the one on the sideline encouraging his teammates, rallying them and getting them to go out there and turn the game around."

Mahomes was only 24 years old but groomed for moments like this. His father Pat and godfather LaTroy Hawkins were longtime Major League Baseball pitchers. Mahomes didn't exactly grow up in a pro sports locker room but spent enough time in one as a youngster to understand how things work. Hawkins recalled a time in 2008 when he was pitching for the Houston Astros that president George W. Bush visited the clubhouse before a game. Hawkins remembered looking over at one point to see a 12-year-old Mahomes chatting up the president. "You should have seen the way he handled himself with the president of the United States," Hawkins said. "He wasn't in awe of who he was. He was just having a conversation with the president like he was old enough to vote, or it was something that happened every day. He's just always been a mature person."

That manifested itself in the playoffs when he led the Chiefs back from 24–0 against the Texans and back from 17–7 against the Tennessee Titans in the next week's AFC Championship Game and back from 20–10 in the fourth quarter of Super Bowl LIV against the San Francisco 49ers. "It doesn't seem like any moment has been too big for him, so I don't know why that would change now," Chiefs tackle Mitchell Schwartz said. "Pretty much everything that's [been] thrown at him through the year, he's handled really well. I think he gets more excited for these games than anything. I've never seen him be nervous or anxious or any of that. I think he's always just ready and excited to show himself and really lead this team. He's a different guy. He's a special guy. He grew up around sports his whole life. This is what he was kind of meant to do in a way."

Mahomes' father put him on that path. "As soon as he could walk, pretty much, I started taking him to the ballpark," Pat Mahomes said. "He got to be a part of it. He got to dress in a uniform, go out on the field before the game. He was probably 5 years old and caught his first ball in batting practice off a big league bat. He's always been a student of whatever game he was playing. He always wanted to learn. For him to get to be around me and around my teammates and see what we went through every day, that had a big influence on him.

He learned how to act like a professional athlete and he takes that with him now every day."

Patrick Mahomes recalled watching Alex Rodriguez, one of his father's teammates with the Texas Rangers, practice long before a game would begin. "My favorite player growing up was Alex Rodriguez," Mahomes said. "I remember how hard Alex worked. That really stuck with me. You see him hitting off the tee for hours and you're like, 'Man, you're hitting home runs every single game. Why are you hitting on the tee for two or three hours?' That's just stuff you see and you remember as a kid, and it sticks with you."

But his early exposure to professional athletes doesn't explain everything. He is just one of those people who seems to thrive in high-pressure situations. In 2018, his first season as a starter, Mahomes had an NFL-high QBR of 74.7 when throwing under pressure. Some of the NFL's best veteran quarterbacks—Tom Brady, Drew Brees, Aaron Rodgers, Russell Wilson, were far below that, and the league average was 21.0.

In 2019 Mahomes' under-pressure QBR was 65.1, which ranked second in the NFL and well above the league average of 17.1. Mahomes in 2018, in particular, thrived outside the pocket. That season he threw 14 touchdown passes and for 996 yards, the most in both categories for a quarterback outside the pocket in the previous 10 seasons.

The game seems to slow down for Mahomes in the heat of a moment in a way it doesn't for most others. "He doesn't get fazed by anything," Schwartz said. "There's nothing too high or too low. He's pretty steady. It's kind of a cool attribute. He plays with emotion and he plays with passion. Usually when that happens, you see good and bad, high and low. When things go bad, you see he is frustrated with himself, but…he's excited for the next opportunity to go better himself. That's special from anyone—let alone someone so young."

When Mahomes was deciding in 2017 whether to leave college with eligibility remaining to declare for the NFL draft, Hawkins sat him down to explain what the move would mean for a young quarterback. "I wanted him to understand that he was going to be the young guy in the clubhouse, and he was going to have to lead grown men," Hawkins said, "not college kids all his age but grown men, whose production determines whether they're going to feed their families. I asked him whether he was ready to do that, whether he was ready to tell a nine-year veteran to shut up and quit complaining about not getting the ball and stop poisoning everything good that's going on. He didn't hesitate. He looked at me and said, 'I'm ready to lead men.'"

Mahomes arrived in Kansas City as the backup to an established veteran in Alex Smith. He immediately understood his place in the locker room and tried his best to blend in with the surroundings—perhaps a tribute to a solid support system that includes his father, his mother Randi, Hawkins, and agents Leigh Steinberg and Chris Cabot. The process of Mahomes becoming a locker-room leader began almost immediately last year after the Chiefs traded Smith to the Washington Redskins. "He just took control out there on the first day," Travis Kelce said. "That's the biggest thing is seeing that he does have control of the room at such a young age, knowing this was his first rodeo in the NFL. He's not shy about taking the lead, and that's huge. It makes it easier on all of us to see the direction of where this can go and it's easy to follow that. Every single throw, it means something to him. Every single play means something to him. He's not going to just sit there or lie down, knowing he's got two 300-pounders in his face. He's going to go ahead and try to make both of them miss—and still make a throw to get us in position to keep the ball going down the field."

Mahomes took immediate command of a locker room that at the time included established voices like like Kelce, Justin Houston, and Eric Berry. That can be tricky for a young player, but Mahomes didn't seem intimidated by the task. "I don't see anything as intimidating," Mahomes said. "That just comes with the relationship you build with the guys off the field and on the field. Whenever you have respect for each other and you know that you're trying to make the team the best you can and you know he's trying to make the team win, you can talk to each other and say things to each other and you respect that. That comes with all of this offseason work, the weight room, the running. If you're giving it your all every single day, people will respect you and respect whenever you say anything on the field."

That process was seamless. It's just something that Mahomes does. "He's been doing this since he was a 9-year-old shortstop on a 12-year-old team," Hawkins said. "This is what he's made for: to be in positions like this. The only time I've ever seen him lose his composure was in a college game after somebody hit him late. He thought it was a cheap shot. I've seen him talk some trash after that. But even in high school, when everybody was coming at him because he was this great athlete, he just never got baited into that. He always just let his play do the talking. He's never been in an environment when he didn't thrive. He's comfortable in uncomfortable situations. Where other people let the situations control them, he always controls the situation."

The situation for Mahomes and the Chiefs was grim when they were down 24–0 to the Texans. That's when Mahomes urged his teammates to take advantage of the opportunity. "Obviously, we didn't want to be in that spot, but I think the biggest thing I was preaching to the team was, 'Let's go do something special,'" he said. "'Everybody is already counting us out. Let's just go play by play and put our best effort out there.' Obviously, I knew that as a team everything had to go the right way. I thought the defense stepped up. The special teams stepped up. Offensively, we started making the plays we weren't making and play by play we just chipped away at that lead. Then we go to the half and then in the second half we kept firing. When you are down 24–0 in the NFL, you don't win a lot of those games. We knew it was still early in the game, first quarter pretty much, and there was a lot of game left. I thought the best thing was seeing everybody's attitude. Everybody obviously wasn't happy, but they knew that we were going to find a way to fight until the end. I thought that was the biggest thing you could see on our sideline. Guys wanted another chance to get out there and play."

Andy Reid said, "You saw him going up and down the bench. He was talking to everybody saying, 'Let's just settle down and go.' As a head coach, you can't ask for more than that. He's just going 'Hey, listen, we're going to be fine. Let's go. Let's not wait until the fourth quarter. Let's go now.' He did that [on the sideline]."

Until Mahomes became their starter in 2018, almost every time the Chiefs readied themselves for a playoff game in the previous 25 years, they had more reason to fear the rival quarterback than their opponent. Those fears, it turned out, were not unfounded. Before Mahomes entered the lineup, the Chiefs had lost 11 of their previous 12 postseason games, dating back to January 1994, in large part because their opponents almost always had the superior quarterback, who was often one of the game's greats. The Chiefs lost eight games to quarterbacks who are either in the Pro Football Hall of Fame or who should get there eventually. This list includes Peyton Manning (twice), Tom Brady, John Elway, Dan Marino, and Jim Kelly.

The Chiefs countered occasionally with good players like Alex Smith, Trent Green, and an end-of-his-career Joe Montana but also with journeymen such as Steve Bono, Elvis Grbac, and Matt Cassel. It's no wonder the Chiefs at times felt intimidated before kickoff. This quarterback deficit wasn't something the Chiefs talked about, but it hung over them like a dark cloud. "That conversation never occurred," former offensive assistant coach Brad Childress said. "Maybe that was because it was just understood, but it never got verbalized. We just didn't go there. Offensively, we were more worried about what we had to do against their defense to be able to be successful. In some cases we were and in other cases we weren't."

The Chiefs even sometimes resorted to rooting for cold weather for their playoff games in the hope that wind, snow, or ice might be the great equalizer among the starting quarterbacks. Green recalled being disappointed with a 50-degree Kansas City afternoon for a January 2004 playoff game against the Indianapolis Colts at Arrowhead Stadium. "We thought we were going to get weather in the 20s and windy," Green said. "We knew at the time, at that stage of his career, Peyton didn't have a high success rate playing outside in the cold. We were excited about that. I knew that day when I woke up it was going to have to be a shootout, and we as an offense were going to have to hold up our end of the bargain because of the way it was."

He was right. Manning threw for 304 yards and three touchdowns, and the Colts never had to punt. The Chiefs couldn't quite keep up and lost 38–31.

The Chiefs may have never drafted Mahomes based solely on what Smith accomplished in the regular season. He was 50–26 as a starter and helped the Chiefs win two AFC West championships in five seasons. But he was 1–4 for the Chiefs in the playoffs. He did deliver that lone victory among the Chiefs' 12 pre-Mahomes playoff games—a 30–0 win against the Texans in January 2016—but Houston helped the Chiefs that day by starting their own journeyman quarterback, Brian Hoyer.

The Chiefs' pessimism about the quarterback matchup in the playoffs disappeared by the time Mahomes started his first postseason game in January 2019 against the Colts in the divisional round, even though Indianapolis quarterback Andrew Luck was coming off a big season of his own. "The way he's started his career, it's unlike any other in NFL history," Green said. "When you have that kind of quarterback, you never think you're out of a game."

Against the Colts, Mahomes and the Chiefs broke a six-game home playoff game losing streak, which dated back 25 years. The next week they had a fourth-quarter lead in the AFC Championship Game against the New England Patriots, but they couldn't hold on and eventually lost in overtime. That loss did little to diminish the Chiefs' optimism going into the Texans' playoff game even against an opposing quarterback like Deshaun Watson.

After all, Mahomes has proven to be a quick study. "He's shown to be even more than we thought he would be during the draft process," Hunt said. "We knew he had the ability to make [unconventional] plays, but what we didn't expect was that he would learn the offense as quickly as he has, learn how to read defenses, be able to operate coach Reid's offense, which is very complicated. In so many ways he's exceeded our expectations. When you have a guy like Patrick under center, you have a chance to win every game."

The Chiefs won their final six regular-season games in 2019 but hadn't scored in big numbers during the streak. They topped 30 points only twice—once with the help of a defensive touchdown and another time after scoring on a kickoff return. But they had the offensive punch against the Texans when they had to have it. "The biggest thing is when you have guys like Tyreek Hill, Travis Kelce, Sammy Watkins, and Mecole Hardman, you know you can score points," Mahomes said. "It's just about the flow of the game. I think I've been saying this for the last five or 10 or whatever games: you have to read how the game is going. Obviously, with how we started the game, the offense, defense, and special teams knew we had to score points. That meant more scrambling around, taking more chances, taking more shots, and I thought guys made a lot of plays. It was an amazing thing. Everything was working. The plays and calls were great. Everyone was getting open against man coverage, which we have been preaching all year long, and guys were making plays."

On defense Clark led the way with three sacks. He wasn't at his best in the Week Six game against the Texans because he was bothered by a pinched nerve in his neck. He took that loss—and a big game from Texans running back Carlos Hyde, who was on the Chiefs' roster during training camp—personally. He jawed with Hyde throughout the game and seemed to take pride that he led the defensive effort in ending the Texans' season. "The last time they were here they beat us, just smacked us in the face," Clark said. "That's the one thing I remember. At the end of the day, they're talking to the wrong guy, talking to the wrong team. They come in here talking all that stuff and they come out here, and we embarrass them. We sent them home early. I hope they enjoy their offseason."

The Chiefs turned their attention to the following week's AFC Championship Game against the Titans, who beat the No. 1 seed Baltimore Ravens in the other divisional round playoff game to allow the Chiefs to play the conference title game at Arrowhead Stadium rather than have to travel to Baltimore. The Chiefs were back in the AFC title game for the second straight year, but the pressure to reach the Super Bowl was greater than in 2018. Then, the Chiefs were facing not only a dynasty in the Patriots, but also two of the greatest of all time at their craft in Brady and coach Bill Belichick. The Chiefs' 2018 season was a great one regardless of whether they reached the Super Bowl or not.

The 2019 season was different. No longer was it acceptable for their season to end in the AFC Championship Game, particularly against the Titans, who finished the regular season at 9–7. The season was a bust at this point if the Chiefs didn't reach Super Bowl LIV. "Obviously, it's an amazing accomplishment first off to be in the AFC championship," Mahomes said. "At the beginning of the season, you have all these goals, and it's a process. Obviously, we're very excited we get to play in the AFC championship and get to play it at home with the home fans. But now we're just going into it with the mentality of not coming up short. We've played the Titans, and they're a great football team. We know it's going to be a great challenge, so we're excited to get in there and prepare ourselves in order to go out and play our best football. Being in the AFC championship, we're going to put the pressure on ourselves to find a way to win it. When you fall that short and that close last year, the next step is to get to the Super Bowl. We understood that going into this season and we know it's a long season. We know it's a process. We know that day by day we have to get better. I think that's what this team is great at: just getting better every single day and then going out and fighting until the end in every single opportunity we get."

The Chiefs would be facing the Titans, another opponent that had beaten them during the regular season. Clark didn't seem to have the same animosity for the Titans as he did for the Texans. But he did remember the earlier game's result. "We owe them one," he said.

19

THE LAMAR HUNT TROPHY

"This is a very special day for our family and the entire organization. We were thrilled to host the AFC Championship Game last year and, as Andy said, we came up four inches short. The job that the franchise did, the team did, the coaches did in terms of getting back to this game and to host at Arrowhead, I thought was tremendous. Obviously, we are very emotional. We are very excited to win the trophy that has my dad's name on it and have an opportunity to head to Miami and head to Super Bowl LIV."
—Chairman Clark Hunt after the Chiefs beat the Tennessee Titans at Arrowhead Stadium to advance to the franchise's first Super Bowl in 50 years.

SHORTLY AFTER HE JOINED THE KANSAS CITY CHIEFS in a trade from the Seattle Seahawks, defensive end Frank Clark talked about the kind of player his new team would be getting. "I bring a unique set of abilities," Clark said. "I bring a type of attitude and swagger with my play that I feel like every coach loves and I feel like my teammates will love. I feel like it's infectious. When you can play and make plays on the field and then bring other players with you, I feel like that's the key. I feel that's when you become a great player. Not just about your individual stats, but when you can contribute and help in a whole other manner, which helps out players on your team, that's when I feel like you're doing your job."

Clark wasn't a huge contributor during the first half of the regular season. He looked more talk than action as he had one sack in the Chiefs' first six games before missing two more with a pinched nerve in his neck. That was hardly what the Chiefs expected when they traded their first-round draft pick and a second rounder in 2020 and then signed Clark to a five-year contract worth more than $100 million.

Clark then turned his season around about the time the Chiefs started to play well defensively, and there was no coincidence between the two developments. Clark had seven sacks over his final eight regular-season games. And then the playoffs were the time Clark truly and consistently became the player he described and the one the Chiefs thought they were getting. He effectively ended the AFC Championship Game and gave the Chiefs their biggest victory in 50 years when he sacked Tennessee Titans quarterback Ryan Tannehill for a 17-yard loss on fourth down late in the fourth quarter. "Just effort," Clark said of the sack. "My whole life is based on effort. Go hard on every play and never give up. I'm just trying to go out there and prove myself to everybody and show who is one of the best defensive ends in the world is."

The Chiefs beat the Titans 35–24 because they were able to do something they hadn't done in a Week 10 loss to Tennessee, which was limit the production of running back Derrick Henry. In the earlier game, Henry rushed for 188 yards, and 140 yards and both of his touchdowns came in the second half. The Chiefs were left exhausted physically after an afternoon of trying to tackle Henry.

Going into the AFC Championship Game, they sounded drained emotionally at the mere prospect of having to try it again. "It's going to take a lot of us hitting him and tackling him, more than one guy," linebacker Anthony Hitchens said. "You've got to take his legs out. We've talked all week about killing the engine, hitting him in his legs and thighs, and chopping him down. When you tackle him high, he tends to carry you for about five more yards."

The Chiefs didn't have many defenders remaining from 2017, but those who were still around remember Henry running for 114 yards and a touchdown in the second half of a wild-card round playoff game. Henry's running helped the Titans erase a 21–3 halftime deficit and beat the Chiefs 22–21.

Henry's big second-half performances weren't limited to when he faced the Chiefs. He led the NFL in the regular season in rushing in 2019 with 1,540 yards. Almost 1,000 of those yards came after halftime. He had 76 rushing yards in the second half of Tennessee's wild-card round win against the New England Patriots and 139 in the second half of the Titans' divisional round win against the Baltimore Ravens.

The Titans wouldn't give up on Henry even when they were behind. They trailed the Chiefs 29–20 in the fourth quarter of the Week 10 game when Tennessee started a drive at its 25. The situation called for the Titans to be in a passing mode, but they ran on nine of the drive's 10 plays. Henry carried seven times for 26 yards and scored a one-yard touchdown to bring the Titans within two points. "The most important thing is we've got to finish the game strong," Tyrann Mathieu said. "If you watch a lot of Derrick Henry, he gets stronger as the game goes on. His first halves, they aren't that great, but second-half football, he takes off."

The Chiefs improved their rush defense significantly since facing the Titans and Henry in Week 10. They allowed an average of 148 rushing yards in the first 10 games but 95 yards in the seven games since. But their defense hadn't faced a rushing threat in those seven games like the one they would see from Henry and the Titans. "The mentality is that somebody is going to have to stop him," Mathieu said. "Somebody is going to have to make a tackle on him if we want to get to Miami."

The Chiefs had 13 possessions in their previous playoff game against the Houston Texans and sounded as if they were preparing for a lesser number in the AFC title game. The more production Henry would get, the fewer chances the high-scoring Chiefs' offense figured to receive. The Chiefs scored 51 points against Houston, at one point scoring a touchdown on seven straight possessions and then adding a field goal on the eighth. "It's important for us to make sure we're maximizing the opportunities that are presented to us," offensive coordinator Eric Bieniemy said before the AFC Championship Game. "It's important for us to take care of business on our side of the ball. It is important for us to execute with great attention to details and it is important for us to put points on the board to apply pressure to them."

Defensive coordinator Steve Spagnuolo knew the challenge his unit faced. "Somehow, someway, we've got to find a way to get them to third down and then win third down," Spagnuolo said. "If we don't do that, we can't get the ball back to Patrick Mahomes and Coach Reid. That's going to be the challenge we're going to have."

Clark was the one Chiefs player publicly confident the Chiefs would control Henry. In an interview with NFL Network two days before the game, Clark said the challenge of stopping Henry wasn't an imposing one. "He's not hard to hit," Clark said. "He's just a big guy, 240, 245, 250. Honestly, he should be running harder at his weight and at his size. I don't see difficulty in tackling him…He's just easy to me up front because I don't look at any running back like they can't be tackled. He's not one of the best guys at breaking tackles to me, honestly."

Clark set up the Chiefs for failure, but they backed up his words. Henry got off to a quick start with 62 yards in the first half. He had just seven after that. "It just comes with execution," Clark said afterward. "That's why I spoke so confidently…because I knew what we were going to do. I knew how much work we had put into stopping the run. That's why I felt so confident. We went out there and we got the job done."

Clark had three sacks in the previous week's win against the Texans in the divisional round. That set a Chiefs playoff record. He also ended Houston's final possession with a fourth-down sack, but his most spectacular play came earlier, when he simply wouldn't quit on a third-quarter play that resulted in a sack of Texans quarterback Deshaun Watson. On that play Clark made a couple of attempts at Watson but failed to get him and even fell to the ground at one point. But he got up and wound up making the tackle.

The Chiefs needed a big game from Clark against the Texans since they played without Chris Jones, their leader in sacks during the regular season. Jones missed the game with a sore calf, and the Texans had beaten the Chiefs in October when Jones didn't play. It was one of two games during the season, in which the Chiefs failed to register a sack. Led by Clark's effort, this time the Chiefs had five sacks.

Clark's work ethic is in part a result of his difficult upbringing. He and his mother spent time in homeless shelters. "It comes from coming from the bottom," Clark said. "Where I come from, there's not a lot of opportunities to do things like this: to go out here and have fun with my teammates and play football in front of these great fans. I stayed in shelters, I stayed in people's homes, I stayed in bus stops across the world, me and my mom. So at the end of the day I'm just thankful for the opportunity…and just loving every opportunity."

Clark likes to say he can speak things into existence, but he knew he couldn't talk himself into a big game in the Super Bowl. San Francisco 49ers quarterback Jimmy Garoppolo gets rid of the ball too quickly for that. So Clark settled for making one of the game's biggest defensive plays instead. His sack of Garoppolo—the Chiefs' only sack of the game—on fourth down with less than 90 seconds to play gave the Chiefs the ball back. Two plays later Damien Williams turned a four-point lead into 11 and sealed their first Super Bowl championship in 50 years.

If Mathieu's voice was the one of reason on the defensive side for the Chiefs, Clark's was the one of inspiration. He was asked if he doubted the Chiefs' ability to rally when they were behind the 49ers by 10 points in the fourth quarter "Never," Clark said. "I don't doubt [anything], man. We were down 24–0 against the Texans, and in that game, I said we were going to go hit them in the mouth. And what happened? We end up hitting them in the mouth. This game… we were down 10 points, and it's 15 minutes to go, and then [49ers players] start celebrating football like they were about to win the

Super Bowl. I went out there next drive and said, 'Y'all's going home too, like the rest of them.'"

The Chiefs' other major free-agent acquisition, Mathieu, came to the Chiefs early in the offseason. He signed shortly after free agency began. The Chiefs had to be patient in order to obtain Clark. He had no contract with the Seahawks, but they retained his rights by designating him as their franchise player. The Chiefs in the meantime cleared out roster room for Clark by ridding themselves of their two longtime edge rushers, Justin Houston and Dee Ford. Houston was released, and Ford was traded to the 49ers for a 2020 second-round pick, which they would need to get Clark. A couple of days before the draft, the Chiefs and Seahawks agreed to terms of the trade. "A trade of this magnitude would only be done if we felt he was elite," general manager Brett Veach said. "He is one of the very best defensive football players in the National Football League. He can win with speed, he can win with power, he can win inside as a rusher, he can win outside as a rusher, he's dominant against the run. He has almost no weaknesses to his game.

"Then when you throw in all those factors and you watch him play, he does it every single down. He's not gassing up for the fourth quarter. He starts the game and he ends the game in the same fashion. He just keeps coming and coming and coming. When this process started, and we made the moves we did and moved on from Justin and Dee, this was the plan. Our plan was to try to get Frank Clark. I told the guys, 'Look, I don't know if we're going to be able to get him. If Seattle doesn't tag him, he's going to cost a lot of money, right? If they do tag him, we're going to have to have some equity to get him.' This was our plan all along. This was a guy we targeted, and you know I'm rather persistent. When we find someone we like, we find a way to go get him. We did that with Patrick [too]."

Unlike Mahomes, who was an immediate star after becoming a starter, the Chiefs' investment in Clark didn't play off until later in the season. Clark's first breakthrough came in the Week 11 win against the Los Angeles Chargers in Mexico City. There he hounded Philip Rivers with five pressures. He hit Rivers as he threw on one of those plays, and the result was an interception. He also had a strip sack of Rivers in the fourth quarter.

Clark also had a big game against the run. He forced the Chargers to punt in the fourth quarter after he tackled running back Austin Ekeler for a one-yard loss on a third-down play. "That was as important a play as any," Spagnuolo said. "That's basically what we've been preaching here, and we always do: situational awareness and disciplined play as you venture into November and December. It's very important."

Clark wasn't productive early in the season in part because he was playing with a pinched nerve in his neck. He, though, stayed patient during the early season, always believing better times were ahead. "I'm a pro," Clark said. "I know everything isn't going to be in my favor all the time. I know that opens up doors for other people. They've got to make the play when it's there. I know what I bring. I know what I bring to the table. I know what other teams are going to do. They can keep it coming. I'm going to keep it coming too."

Later in the season, he was bothered by a stomach ailment that limited his playing time in a couple of games. Clark said he began the season around 260 pounds, but at one point during his illness, his weight had dropped to 238. He played through the ailment because the Chiefs needed him. Two of their top defensive ends, Alex Okafor and Emmanuel Ogbah, were lost for the season because of injuries. The Chiefs faced the New England Patriots and Denver Broncos in Weeks 14 and 15 and had yet to acquire veteran defensive end Terrell Suggs, who was claimed off waivers from the Arizona Cardinals for the final two regular-season games and the playoffs.

Clark also insisted on playing more during this stretch than the Chiefs planned. "We started off slowly with him, but he gets very aggravated with that," Andy Reid said. "So you're better off just letting him get in and go. The fact he played as well as he did amazed me. This kid loves to play the game. I know he wasn't feeling well and then for him to come out there. I wasn't sure exactly how many snaps he was going to be able to play. But he was bound and determined to get out there."

Clark's stomach problems at one point caused him to seek help from a specialist and spend a night in a Kansas City hospital. But he was a factor against the Patriots by getting a sack and another tackle for negative yardage. He didn't get a sack against the Broncos but hit Denver quarterback Drew Lock twice.

He eventually regained the weight he lost. "Week after week I'm just going to keep on building until I get back to the point where I feel I need to be," Clark said. "When I started the season off, I was probably at 20 percent [effectiveness]. I had a lot of doctors tell me I shouldn't even start the season. I shouldn't even have been playing. I just wanted to go out there from the start of the season and just show my teammates and prove to Chiefs [fans] that I'm here to stay and that they know what type of player they're getting in me. There was a lot going on that was slowing me down that wasn't allowing me to be myself…The type of player I am, I like to play wild. I like to play with a lot of aggression. I play with a lot of flash. Everything comes with confidence with me. That's how it starts. I feel like I'm the best player on the field when I'm on the field. I've got a lot of things to prove. I feel I'm one of the best defensive ends in the league and I feel I want to be the best when it's all said and done. When you eliminate injuries, then it just comes down to ability. When you put my ability against any offensive tackle in the league, I choose myself over every offensive tackle."

Once healthy and playing full games toward the end of the regular season and in the playoffs, Clark backed up his words. "I'm just happy that's all out of the way now and I get to actually go back to playing football," Clark said late in the season. "Just being in the hospital and having to get all of these tests done, that's taken a toll on my energy. It feels good to get back to normal with my teammates. [Opponents have] got to keep it coming because I'm going to keep it coming. My neck and a lot of that other stuff is in the past now. So they're getting some football from Frank Clark."

After Clark helped the Chiefs win the AFC Championship Game, the Arrowhead Stadium field was littered with confetti, Clark Hunt got to hoist the AFC championship trophy named for his father and the Chiefs' founder, Lamar Hunt. It was the Chiefs' first AFC championship. As he accepted it, Clark Hunt reflected on the franchise's dry spell of 50 years without a Super Bowl appearance. "The journey is a big part of it," Hunt said. "We are going to celebrate tonight, and it is going to be tremendous. It would not be what it is without the hardship, without all of the hard work that went into getting us here. Fifty years is too long, but we are going to Miami. We have a chance to win another Super Bowl. It was heartbreaking [to lose in the AFC Championship Game the year before], but we were playing a franchise that has been tremendously successful over the last decade plus. And there was probably a questions mark in the back of our heads to whether we could really beat them because it had been so many times where you thought the Patriots were out, but sure enough, they found a way to win it and go on to win the Super Bowl. I think the experience of having played in the game last year helped the entire organization, particularly the players and coaches. I think they had a little bit more confidence coming into today. They knew what to expect. Although we didn't get off with quite as fast of a start as I would have liked, they responded pretty quickly. We were able to get the lead as we went into the second half."

Hunt received the trophy after the game from former linebacker Bobby Bell, who played on the Chiefs' Super Bowl IV championship team. Bell was a member of a national championship team in college at the University of Minnesota and was a champion as a professional as well. He is a member of the Pro Football Hall of Fame and was named one of the NFL's top 100 all-time players. But Bell said presenting the Lamar Hunt Trophy to Lamar's son was at the top of his list of personal achievements. "Lamar and I were really close," Bell said of Hunt, who died in 2006. "He was like a dad to me."

The Chiefs, who were moving on the play the NFC champion 49ers in Super Bowl LIV, had no bigger fans than Bell and the other members of the 1969 Chiefs. Several players from that team—most in their 70s and 80s and some coming from distant places like Virginia, Louisiana, and Texas—braved windchill in the single digits to be in Kansas City to watch the Chiefs beat the Titans.

Loyalty to Lamar Hunt and his family is a reason many of the former Chiefs are so interested in seeing the modern team do well. That's particularly true for African American players like Bell and fellow Hall of Fame linebacker Willie Lanier. Because opportunities for black football players in the 1950s and 1960s weren't always available, Bell went from his childhood home in North Carolina to Minnesota to play in college. Lanier stayed closer to his home in Virginia but played for a historically black college at Morgan State. Back in those days, jobs in professional football were difficult to come by for African American players. "That's why we're all happy for the Hunt family," Lanier said. "With Lamar being who he was and with his interest in having a wonderful, diversified roster, we were able to go forth and do the things we did. The Hunt family and the American Football League created employment for gentlemen from historically black colleges. They gave us the opportunity."

Lanier was supposed to present the Lamar Hunt Trophy to Clark Hunt in 2018 after the AFC Championship Game, but the Chiefs lost to the Patriots in overtime. "It's disappointing that I never got that chance," Lanier said. "It was a chance to appreciate the person who was the architect, the leader, the man who made it all happen. You have to acknowledge all the Hunt family has done for so many people."

The Chiefs had many lean seasons since their last Super Bowl appearance, leading the 79-year-old Bell and others to wonder whether they would live long enough to see their former team in another Super Bowl. "I thought I would have to go back to playing for them," Bell said. "I thought I'd have to put the uniform back on."

Lanier missed the victory parade in Kansas City after Super Bowl IV. He was one of 11 Chiefs who returned with the team to Kansas

City from New Orleans, site of Super Bowl IV, but then turned right around for Houston, where they participated in the last AFL All-Star Game. "That was a piece of the puzzle that makes winning that Super Bowl incomplete," he said. "I saw wonderful pictures of the parade and I feel we missed out a part of the whole experience."

Jack Steadman, then the Chiefs general manager, apologized to Lanier and the others for not including them in the parade. "He told me the next time we went to the Super Bowl, he would let us come back to Kansas City and be a part of the parade and other festivities and then go to the All-Star Game," Lanier said. "We never got that chance. So if the Chiefs win this year, I'll be in Kansas City for the parade."

And Lanier did indeed attend the victory parade when the Chiefs beat the 49ers.

20

WIN ONE FOR ANDY

"I'm happy for the Hunt family most of all. They've been through a lot over the years. For them to have this [Lombardi Trophy] back in their hands I think is tremendous. And for the city of Kansas City, it's great…And then for our team, I told them I'd coach another 20 years if I could have that group right there. They're a beautiful bunch, resilient, tough, tough-minded, very tough-minded as you saw tonight. I'm so proud of them."

—Andy Reid after Super Bowl LIV.

WHILE THERE WAS PLENTY OF DEBATE about whether the Kansas City Chiefs with Patrick Mahomes and their powerful offense or the San Francisco 49ers with their strong defensive front and No. 1 scoring defense were the better team heading into Super Bowl LIV, there was no doubt about the sentimental favorite to win the game. Seemingly anyone not connected with the 49ers was rooting for Andy Reid, who in his 21st season as an NFL head coach and seventh with the Chiefs had made only one Super Bowl appearance. That one didn't go well, as the Philadelphia Eagles lost to the New England Patriots in Super Bowl XXXIX on February 6, 2005.

The Chiefs gave Reid his elusive Super Bowl victory but spared him no drama in doing it. Before winning the game 31–20, the Chiefs were down by 10 points midway through the fourth quarter. Then their furious rally delivered three touchdowns and heroics from the defense in the form of a turnover on downs and an interception in the game's final seven minutes. Just like that, 50 years of frustration were washed away. "They're going to make a movie out of this," defensive tackle Chris Jones said.

For Reid his second Super Bowl experience as a head coach went more smoothly than the first. With the Eagles trailing by 10 points in that fourth quarter, Philadelphia played with no urgency. The Eagles went on a 13-play drive to get a touchdown, but in doing so, they devoured most of the remaining clock. The Eagles left themselves little time for a tying or winning score and went on to lose to the Patriots 24–21.

Reid is a likable person and seemingly without an NFL enemy. He is loved by many former and current players, which was why "Win one for Andy" was such a big theme in the two weeks leading up to the Super Bowl. Chiefs players made a tribute to Reid on the team's chartered flight from Kansas City to Miami for the game. Many, including Mahomes, Travis Kelce, Tyreek Hill, and Tyrann Mathieu, wore Hawaiian shirts, which is among Reid's favorite leisure apparel. Reid wore a suit and tie for travel, but the message from those playing and coaching with him was clear. "Just getting him [to the Super Bowl] isn't the goal," Kelce said. "Winning this thing for him is."

Indeed, hanging around the Chiefs as they prepared for Super Bowl LIV, it was easy for one to get the feeling players and assistant coaches wanted a victory for Reid more than the head coach wanted one for himself. "Nobody deserves it more than Andy," longtime special teams coordinator Dave Toub said. "He's such a great coach to not have a Super Bowl win under his belt. This would be huge. I don't know if I'd stop crying with him. I'd probably hug him forever. I'm just so proud of what he's done and everything he's done in his career. He needs that."

Reid entered the game as arguably the most accomplished coach in NFL history without a Lombardi Trophy to his credit. He was sixth in all-time wins with 221. Three of the coaches ahead of him worked during the Super Bowl era and won at least two titles. The other two coached before the Super Bowl era but won multiple NFL championships. Then came Reid, who had just the one Super Bowl experience, and it was less than glorious. In the days leading up to the game, he insisted that the missing accomplishment of a Super Bowl championship didn't eat away at him. "Life's bigger than that," the 61-year-old Reid said. "That doesn't tell you I don't want to win. This is America. I'm in it to win. That's what we do. I don't want that to be slighted. But I also understand the perspective of life. Maybe it's because of my age. That doesn't mean I'm not going to work hard and coach hard and do all of those things and come in swinging to the best of my ability. But I'm not going to tell you there aren't other things in life. I understand that, too. I think more of the players than I sit here thinking about myself. That's not where I go."

Those close to him, but not connected to the Chiefs, say not to be fooled. "He understands what this would mean for his career," said Louis Riddick, the ESPN NFL analyst who worked with Reid for five seasons in the Eagles' personnel department. "You don't coach and dedicate yourself in the manner, in which he has, because it's fun. You do it because you're Type A competitive. You don't get to this point where he's gotten to in his profession if you didn't care about legacy.

That's important to him. He wants that on his wall. He's never going to let you in on just how important it is. He's just not that guy who's going to give you that sound bite interview where he says, 'Man, this means everything to me!' But that competitiveness burns in him. I've seen it in different areas and different ways. I know it exists. You don't get to where he is without it."

Reid's playoff history, particularly after he joined the Chiefs, was tortured. His career playoff record entering the Super Bowl was 14–14, and although that .500 winning percentage was better than some Hall of Fame coaches like Bud Grant (.455) and Sid Gillman (.167), it was far down the list of coaches who have worked at least one postseason game and also lagging behind contemporaries such as Bill Belichick (.721) and John Harbaugh (.588).

It's also far below Reid's regular-season win percentage of .618. Reid reached five NFC Championship Games with the Eagles but advanced to the Super Bowl just once. That one Super Bowl had been the fewest for any coach with at least 20 playoff games. Nobody had coached more career postseason games and failed to win multiple Super Bowl championships—let alone one. Reid was asked why his teams hadn't been better in the playoffs. "The further you go in the playoffs, the more you [have to] minimize those mistakes, whether that's scheme or penalties or whatever it might be," he said. "You create your own deal and you go play. We don't worry about all that stuff. It's what happens on that field [that matters]. It's man against man, and you play the game."

While coaching the Chiefs, Reid had been the victim of bad playoff luck. Indianapolis Colts quarterback Andrew Luck scored a touchdown in a 2013 playoff game after a teammate fumbled. The ball took a perfect bounce into Luck's hands. The Colts went on to win by a point.

In the 2017 playoffs, Tennessee Titans quarterback Marcus Mariota had one of his passes batted right back to him by a Chiefs defender. Mariota caught it and ran the ball to the end zone for a touchdown. The Titans went on to win by a point.

He had been the victim of some bizarre officiating. The Chiefs lost what would have been a tying two-point conversion against the Pittsburgh Steelers in the fourth quarter of a 2016 playoff game to a questionable holding call. They forced Mariota to fumble on a sack at a key juncture of that 2017 game, but the officials ruled that his forward progress had been stopped and gave the ball back to the Titans.

Reid had even been a victim of his own player's sloppiness. Linebacker Dee Ford lined up offside during the 2018 AFC Championship Game against the Patriots, negating an interception that would have clinched a victory for the Chiefs. "When you get to the playoffs, you have to have a little good luck, and it seems like Andy hasn't had much of that in the playoffs," said Mike Holmgren, the Green Bay Packers head coach in the 1990s who gave Reid his first NFL coaching job. "You can't have officials making a bad call against you. You can't have injuries to a key player or a couple of key players. You don't want to play against a team that's hitting its stride and is hot at that moment. You need the stars to align sometimes. Sometimes it isn't enough to just bring a good team into the playoffs."

There was little question Reid needed a Super Bowl victory to strengthen his candidacy for the Pro Football Hall of Fame. Only one coach in the Super Bowl era failed to win a league championship but still made the Hall of Fame. That coach, former Chiefs head coach

Marv Levy, took the Buffalo Bills to four consecutive Super Bowls, though they lost them all. Reid may have cared more about his legacy than he let on publicly, but he also enjoys his profession for more than just gamedays. Each week during the season, Reid says he's "looking forward to the challenge" of facing the upcoming opponent. That's his way of saying he's eagerly anticipating matching wits with the opposing coaching staff.

He gave up personnel duties he had with the Eagles when he came to the Chiefs. He told team chairman Clark Hunt he wanted more time to teach his players and be an offensive innovator rather than a personnel evaluator. He enjoys more than just the competition. "That's why so many of these great coaches have not been able to coach for as long as he has or been as fresh and driven as he has been," said Joe Banner, who was the Eagles' president from 1999 to 2012. "I don't think Andy is tracking public opinion. I don't think he's moved by public opinion and I don't think any choice or decision he's ever made in his life was driven by public opinion. In the eyes of some, he probably needs to win a Super Bowl to be considered among the best. That's not what drives him, but it would be gratifying to him."

Winning, of course, is important to Reid. He took the loss to the Patriots in the AFC Championship Game after the 2018 season particularly hard. Even after beating the Titans to win the conference title game in 2019, Reid made reference to Ford's offside penalty late in the fourth quarter of that loss against New England. The penalty nullified a game-sealing Charvarius Ward interception, and Reid reminded everyone by saying his team missed back-to-back Super Bowl appearances by four inches. That's about how far Ford lined up offside. "In all the years I worked with Andy, including the really disappointing ends to some seasons, I never saw him or heard him sound like a particular game really took a toll on him because he's incredibly resilient," Banner said. "But after that game last year was the first time I ever had an interaction with him where I felt like this hit him a little bit harder than these other losses. He's always positive, always has a good energy, the way he carries himself and thinks and talks. That was one of the rare times, and maybe the only time on a football-related issue where I had a conversation with him, and I felt like he's human, and it was really hard for him to take."

With all of this as a backdrop, Reid coached Super Bowl LIV with a sense of urgency he didn't show in his previous title game appearance. In doing so, he was one of the Chiefs' stars in their victory. After initially sending the field-goal team on the field in a fourth-and-1 situation deep in 49ers territory in the first quarter, he had a change of heart and went with Mahomes and the offense. Then he showed some imagination by using a play he stole from—of all places—the 1948 Rose Bowl. Four players in the backfield, including Mahomes, spun to their right, so the snap went instead to the running back, Damien Williams. He gained a first down, and the Chiefs scored their first touchdown on the next play to take a 7–3 lead. "It is a pretty simple play, [but] it has all the razzle dazzle," right tackle Mitchell Schwartz said. "When you look at what [Reid] does, it has all the basic concepts: motions, guys going different directions, put a little speed on the field, a little of ball trickery. It is tough to defend. That play is all about Damien Williams. It is about getting us on track. All the other stuff goes on, and it's just kind of a dive play."

The Chiefs had the play in their book and worked on it in practice all season, but they didn't bust it out until a crucial situation in their biggest game of the year. The play caught Reid's attention when he watched film of that long ago Rose Bowl. Michigan, which won the game 49–0, ran the play against USC. Reid obtained a copy of the game film from his brother, who was later coached in high school by one of USC's players. "We kept working on it every single week and kept executing it and doing it the right way, waiting for the perfect time to call it," Mahomes said. "When we were there, and Coach said it, I was like, 'It's time. So let's do it.'"

Reid and his staff routinely borrowed plays from college teams when they were watching video to prepare for the draft. Even on Saturday nights during the season, as the Chiefs fine-tune their game-plan and go through all of the usual day-before-the-game scenarios, they're keeping one eye on the college games on TV—and not purely for entertainment purposes. "Whatever Saturday night football game is on, we're watching and saying, 'Hey, did you see that play?'" offensive coordinator Eric Bieniemy said. "You're looking at all these different college games and you see certain offenses and seeing teams doing certain things. You can't help but notice some of the ingenuity that's being used at that particular level. It has an influence. Everybody's looking at the college game. At the college level, they're making sure you have to defend every inch of the grass. We want [opposing defenses] to defend every blade of grass."

Reid was probably joking when he suggested the Chiefs had pulled more plays from that long ago Rose Bowl and would use them next season. Then again—given his penchant for finding plays anywhere and making them work in a game—maybe he wasn't. "There's some good stuff in there," Reid said.

Before Mahomes' NFL success, many coaches had complained about the difficulty of teaching a pro offensive system to a college spread quarterback. Reid, though, embraced it. Mahomes rarely had even taken a snap from under center at Texas Tech. "The one great thing about college football today is that these kids are throwing the ball," Reid said. "So it used to be you're getting [college quarterbacks] that weren't throwing the ball, and we complained about that as coaches. Heck, now they're throwing the ball, and we're still complaining. I'm going, 'Hey, bring it on.' We went through the option phase and then the I-formation phase. Now guys are spreading them out, and they're throwing it. That to me is a positive. They're having to read things, get the ball out of their hand, move in the pocket a little bit, and learn things they would have otherwise had to learn here. I think they're a step ahead, although it's a different system."

Reid also had the wisdom in the Super Bowl to listen to Mahomes' play suggestion on a third-and-15 situation in the fourth quarter as the Chiefs trailed by 10 points. Mahomes wanted a play the Chiefs called *23 Jet Chip Wasp*. The call was risky. The 49ers had been pressuring Mahomes most of the game with their pass rush. This particular play required Mahomes to take a deep drop in the pocket against a defensive front full of strong rushers, including end Nick Bosa, who had been dominating his matchup against left tackle Eric Fisher all game. "We were in a bad situation, especially with that pass rush," Mahomes said. "We knew those guys would have their ears pinned back. We needed really good protection. It was a long route."

But they made it work. Mahomes took his deep drop. Fisher took care of Bosa, but 49ers tackle DeForest Buckner looped around end and pressured Mahomes to throw, tackling the quarterback right after he released the ball. It traveled longer in the air than any completed Mahomes pass of the 2019 season—57 yards—and was on target to Hill for a 44-yard gain.

Two plays later Mahomes threw a touchdown pass to Kelce, and the Chiefs then trailed just 20–17 and had momentum.

Super Bowl LIV was full of other stars for the Chiefs. But Mahomes overcame his mediocre start to finish well and was named the game's MVP. Mahomes had just 145 passing yards with an interception through the first three quarters, and reporters asked Jones whether Mahomes' performed as well as usual early in the game. "He ain't got to," Jones said. "He's got this defense. That's what matters. When the defense is playing lights out, the defense steps up and makes a stop. That's all Pat needs. He's going to make something happen, the receiving corps going to make something happen. We put them in a position to make plays, and guess what? They excelled."

Jones was another worthy candidate for the game's MVP. He knocked down three passes, and his pressure on San Francisco quarterback Jimmy Garoppolo on one second-quarter play forced an interception. Jones failed to register a sack and was credited with just one tackle but still had a big impact on the game. All three of the passes he knocked down came in the fourth quarter. And on two of them, the 49ers had an open receiver waiting down the field. "You're at the point of the season where sacks really don't count, and they don't matter," Jones said. "As long as you affect the game in any type of way, that's what matters. As long as you can affect the game to put your team in a position to go out there and make a stop, that's what matters. Sacks, tackles, none of that matters."

Drafted by the Chiefs in the second round in 2016, Jones was a good player for the Chiefs during his first two seasons but became a star the minute he tried out a new pair of gloves for a game against the Jacksonville Jaguars early in the 2018 season. Jones got a sack that day—his first of the season—so he wore the gloves in the subsequent game against the Patriots. He got another sack. So Jones decided he would keep wearing the gloves. He wore the same pair the rest of the season. "My gloves smell like a dead animal, but I won't change them up because I'm very superstitious," Jones said. "I won't change the gloves at all. My teammates hate them. You can smell me coming."

The Chiefs gladly accepted an odorous Jones. He continued his streak of games with at least one sack until it reached 11, which gave him the NFL record. Jones is one of the Chiefs' most superstitious players. During the sack streak, he had to have lunch every Monday with the same two people—fellow Chiefs defensive lineman Xavier Williams and former teammate Jarvis Jenkins—at the same Kansas City chicken restaurant, Mother Clucker, where he would place the same order. "Even if I'm not hungry, I have to get the same meal, which is a chicken sandwich, a milkshake—milkshakes are delicious—two chicken breasts, and three orders of fries," Jones said. "I don't eat all of this. It's just the fact that I got it one time, had success with it, and I feel like if something's not broken, why fix it? I pick through it. Of course, I'm going to finish the shake. The shake is like the best thing ever. Dessert is always the best part of dinner."

It's been obvious the past couple of seasons that Jones hasn't been finishing many meals of that size. He was noticeably slimmer than in his first two seasons with the Chiefs, when he played at about 310 pounds. He was down to about 285 the past two years. "I don't eat pork anymore," Jones said without a trace of longing. "I love bacon. I love breakfast food period. But I stopped eating pork. I eat more fish. I'm like a pescatarian, you could say. I eat a lot of fish and a lot of vegetables. I don't really eat meat. I eat a lot of vegetables. I kind of get full off of vegetables and some type of protein."

Jones led the Chiefs with 15.5 sacks in 2018. He predicted a big season for himself at training camp that summer when he was asked about his sack goal. "Lead the NFL," Jones said without a trace of a smile. "I've been talking about it all summer. I've been voicing it to my teammates. I want to lead the NFL in sacks. I believe that whole-heartedly. You have to speak it to believe it."

Jones didn't wind up leading the league, but he finished third and in doing so announced himself as an NFL star. He skipped the Chiefs' 2019 offseason practice and conditioning program despite having one more season remaining on his contract in hopes of getting an extension from the Chiefs. That didn't happen so Jones reported to camp on time and wound up leading the Chiefs in sacks again with nine.

Damien Williams also could have been voted the MVP of Super Bowl LIV. The veteran running back scored both of the Chiefs' final two touchdowns—one on a five-yard pass that put the Chiefs ahead in the fourth quarter and later on an electrifying 38-yard run that will forever live as one of the big plays in Chiefs history. The play was designed as an inside run because the Chiefs were protecting a four-point lead and merely trying to kill the clock. But Williams didn't emerge from obscurity to become a Super Bowl star by always doing things the way they're drawn up. So after taking the ball from Mahomes, he followed fullback Anthony Sherman, his lead blocker, to the left instead. "Sherm came in the game, and he was like, 'Follow me.' And that's exactly what I did," Williams said. "The run was supposed to go inside, but he went outside, so I went outside. I said, 'Forget it. I'm taking it to the house.'"

Williams, who rushed for 104 yards, didn't mind the MVP award going to another player. He entered the NFL as an undrafted free agent. "I had to fight my way in," he said. He just appreciated having a hand in things. Williams was the second undrafted player to rush for more than 100 yards in a Super Bowl. Dominic Rhodes of the Colts was the first and did it in a Super Bowl XLI victory against the Chicago Bears.

What did irritate Williams was hearing for two weeks about the 49ers' running game. "You try not to pay attention to the media and everything, but it's kind of hard to ignore what they're talking about," Williams said. "Just being able to hear them talk about the 49ers as a whole, as an offense and their run game…They're a great team, and I'm not taking anything away from them. Their run game…to not hear your name or anything and just how we do things on the ground, I pay attention."

Sherman said he sensed a big game coming from Williams. "I talked to him before the game and I knew in his heart he was going to bring it," Sherman said. "You could tell from his very first run that he was going at these guys."

Williams spent the first four NFL seasons playing at Miami's Hard Rock Stadium for the Dolphins, adding another level of satisfaction to his big game. He was nothing but a backup for the Dolphins. "It's crazy," he said. "You spend your first four years here, undrafted. Being able to go to a place like [Kansas City], it's crazy. It doesn't feel real yet. When you get into the league, you think about the Super Bowl, you think about what you would do in it, and for it to be where I started my career at, undrafted, it means a lot."

Williams signed with the Chiefs as a free agent before the 2018 season but played little until late in that season, when the Chiefs released Kareem Hunt, who had been their featured back. Williams replaced Hunt and played well, but because he had mostly been a backup, the Chiefs didn't know whether he could handle the physical responsibility of the demanding job over the course of a long season. "There's a certain challenge that comes with that job," Reid said. "That's a tough position to play. You have to prepare yourself on and off the field."

Unsure about where Williams was headed shortly before the start of the season, the Chiefs signed veteran running back LeSean McCoy, who had starred for Reid early in his career with the Eagles. Williams suffered an injury early in camp. "It's a good early reminder that the little things like stretching and hydration really matter," general manager Brett Veach said. "Those are things elite level players do away from the field. It's just a matter of acclimating his body to that kind of workload. He has to figure out the stuff away from the field: diet, extra treatment, and things like that. Sometimes when you're a guy that has been a role player your entire career, you don't get a lot of wear and tear. There's not a lot of need to stay in the training room and there's not a lot of need to watch exactly what you're putting in your body. Now all of a sudden, you're talking 16, 18, 20 carries a game over the course of a 16, and hopefully, a 19-game season. That will take a toll on you. There's no question about his desire. He's one of the toughest guys on our offense. He just has to make sure he knows that wanting to be that guy on the field—there's another part to that. So I'd say when he has his helmet on, he's ready for this. When he takes it off, that's when he's going to have to grow. To go through the violence and the amount of hits he's going to take, it's a lot different than what he's used to."

Williams' change in preparation included his diet. "I had to change my eating habits," he said before the season. "I actually did this thing where they draw your blood and tell you what's actually necessary for you. I kind of just picked up the workload when I'm working out, doing a little more, doing a little extra because, even though this is my sixth year, I've never had the role of the starter or have had to take the bulk of the reps. I learned I'm allergic to spinach. I can't eat spinach, obviously. It's cool to just kind of learn what you can and can't eat."

Sure enough, Williams still had an injury-filled season. He missed most of training camp because of a hamstring injury. He missed two games at one point during the season because of a knee injury and three games later with a rib injury. Through the first half of the season, he was averaging a measly 2.1 yards per carry.

McCoy played well early in the season but fell from favor at mid-year after a rash of fumbles. The Chiefs tried filling in with Darrel Williams and Spencer Ware, but both had their seasons end with injuries. By then Damien Williams was as healthy as he'd been all season and finally emerged as the player the Chiefs hoped he would be. Between the season's final regular-season game, the two playoff games, and the Super Bowl, Williams had two 100-plus-yard games and scored eight touchdowns.

They weren't MVP candidates, but the Chiefs had other Super Bowl heroes as well. Dustin Colquitt punted just twice in the Super Bowl but was the longest-tenured Chiefs player in 2019, having arrived as a third-round draft pick from Tennessee in 2005. His father Craig (Pittsburgh Steelers) and brother Britton (Denver Broncos) had once punted for Super Bowl-winning teams and for years they teased Colquitt unmercifully about the rings they had and the one he didn't. Dustin Colquitt played for some of the worst Chiefs teams of the previous 50 seasons, enduring two 14-loss and two 12-loss seasons.

He was ready to try his luck with another team as a free agent in 2013 when the Chiefs hired Reid, who talked Colquitt into changing his mind and re-signing with Kansas City. Colquitt hoped then for what indeed would follow on the night of February 2, 2020. Colquitt was suddenly a Super Bowl champion, allowing him to enter the conversation with his father and brother. Colquitt was later released by the Chiefs in April, bringing the Kansas City chapter of his playing career to an end after 15 seasons. No other Chiefs player ever played longer in a Kansas City uniform, and his final game for the Chiefs was Super Bowl LIV.

Another special teams player was also pivotal. That's where Sherman mostly plays, but he is listed as a fullback and threw the key block on Williams' final touchdown run. "I got jacked up like I scored the touchdown," Sherman said. "Are you kidding me? As a fullback to be able to make a block like that and for him to score and to essentially seal the Super Bowl, I don't think I can dream up a better scenario for myself."

EPILOGUE

Aᴛᴛᴇʀ ᴛʜᴇ Kᴀɴsᴀs Cɪᴛʏ Cʜɪᴇғs clinched the AFC West division late in the 2022 season with a victory against the Houston Texans, the celebration in the visitors' locker room at Houston's NRG Stadium carried at least some of the trappings of a real party. Many Chiefs players, for instance, wore division title T-shirts and ballcaps to honor the moment. But this was the Chiefs' seventh straight AFC West title, and otherwise the mood carried much of a been-there, done-that vibe. Quarterback Patrick Mahomes told his teammates they should enjoy their accomplishment for a short time, but once the team charter landed back in Kansas City, it would be time to focus on other things. "We've got bigger goals in mind," Mahomes said in the victorious locker room.

What the Chiefs' Super Bowl LIV win against the San Francisco 49ers, the first world championship for the franchise in 50 years, did for the organization was reset expectations. As long as Mahomes was their quarterback, no longer would anything less than an ending that included a Super Bowl victory make for a successful season. In that sense the Chiefs considered each of the two seasons since to be failures. They followed in 2020 with a lopsided loss in Super Bowl LV to the Tampa Bay Buccaneers and in 2021 with an AFC Championship Game loss to the Cincinnati Bengals—the latter after holding an 18-point lead in the first half.

Against this backdrop, the Chiefs' biggest move entering the 2022 season was a subtraction. They decided that a contract extension for one of the stars of their recent success, wide receiver Tyreek Hill, would be too expensive for them to afford. Hill wanted to be the NFL's highest-paid player at his position, and the Chiefs traded him to the Miami Dolphins, who were all too eager to make it happen for him. The Chiefs and general manager Brett Veach expected there would be a few skeptics about their plan for the season after trading Hill. But they were still puzzled by the many suggestions that perhaps after four straight AFC Championship Game appearances and a Super Bowl title they were in something of a rebuild, would take a step back, and would relinquish their spot at or near the top of the conference's power structure. They were planning all along to make another strong championship run and perhaps return to the Super Bowl for the third time in four seasons. "When you have Pat Mahomes, we're wired to go after it every year," Veach said.

Sure enough, the 2022 season finished with the Chiefs holding another championship victory parade. This one happened after the Chiefs overcame a 10-point halftime deficit to win one of the most thrilling Super Bowls ever: a 38–35 victory against the Philadelphia Eagles with the winning points coming on a Harrison Butker field goal with eight seconds remaining. They won it all again not in spite of the trade of Hill—but because of it. The benefits of the deal—many hidden initially in light that the Chiefs were losing such a dynamic wide receiver—revealed themselves as the season went on.

The Chiefs began the 2022 offseason with two major goals. One was to fortify a defense that had aged and lost a step or two since helping to beat the 49ers in Super Bowl LIV. Another was to extend Hill's contract. Then Christian Kirk, a wide receiver who hadn't topped 80 catches in any of his four seasons with the Arizona Cardinals, signed a four-year, $72 million contract with the Jacksonville Jaguars, signaling the market at Hill's position was about to explode. Later, the Green Bay Packers traded Davante Adams to Las Vegas, where he signed a four-year contract worth $28 million per season with the Raiders. Adams' contract became the new target for Hill, making it obvious before the start of free agency in 2022 that Hill's new extension was going to make it difficult for the Chiefs to fulfill both of their offseason goals. So the Chiefs had a decision to make about which way to proceed. Signing Hill to the lucrative contract extension would have come at a cost for the Chiefs, one they would have had trouble in overcoming. The cap number for Mahomes jumped in 2022 to more than $35 million, up from less than $8 million in 2021.

The Chiefs projected their salary cap for years with a potential Hill extension and didn't like what they saw. "Everyone knew what the next two or three years would look like and how many players we'd have to potentially cut and how difficult things would be," Veach said. "We would have had a lot of expensive players. It's hard to be successful in this league year after year. It's hard to win games year after year. There are going to be moments where we have to step out there and do something uncomfortable. No one wanted to lose Tyreek. He's a great player. But if you're going to do something, trust the process and trust how you do things and don't be afraid to commit to change a year sooner when you have more ability to potentially make those changes work better."

The Chiefs eventually opted to revamp their defense rather than re-sign Hill. It's silly to suggest the Chiefs wouldn't have won the Super

Bowl if they decided to re-sign Hill. He had career highs with 119 catches and 1,710 yards during his first year with the Dolphins. But in return the Chiefs received five draft picks from the Dolphins plus some salary-cap flexibility. In the free-agent market, they signed two players who would become starters: JuJu Smith-Schuster and Marquez Valdes-Scantling. The two combined during the regular season for 120 catches and 1,620 yards, numbers similar to those that Hill gave the Dolphins. The combined salary-cap cost for the two was less than $8 million. Valdes-Scantling had a Hill-like performance in the AFC Championship Game win against the Bengals with six catches, 116 yards, and a touchdown.

Just as important were the five draft picks obtained from the Dolphins, including selections in the first, second, and fourth rounds in 2022. The Chiefs turned those picks into a cornerback, Trent McDuffie, and a wide receiver, Skyy Moore. McDuffie was an immediate starter, and Moore scored a touchdown in the Super Bowl win against the Eagles. In addition to McDuffie, the Chiefs covered a lot of ground on defense in the draft. Six rookies played significant roles on that side of the ball. Included were defensive end George Karlaftis, who had six sacks, and cornerback Jaylen Watson, who had an interception in the AFC championship Game victory against the Bengals.

Mahomes initially wasn't a fan of the Hill trade, but it wasn't a tough sell for the Chiefs to convince him it would work both in the short and long term. "I wanted to keep him, for sure," Mahomes said. "They had a plan for it, though. They told me the plan, and we were going to get these draft picks. We were going to go out there and bring in some free-agent receivers, and I think they executed on that. We know that to keep having success in this league we have to keep evolving, keep getting better. I always want to be successful this year, but at the same time, I'm here for the long haul. If we're going to have a long time here, I want to have a chance to win Super Bowls every single year."

Tight end Travis Kelce said he had some initial concerns after the Hill trade, too, including how effective the Chiefs might be on offense and what it all might mean for him. "Yes, that was a question," Kelce said during the 2022 season. "But once I saw how hard guys were working, paying attention to details, how Pat keeps progressing as a quarterback…Right now, we're in a good routine that we just keep getting better. You could feel that from the day we started from May until now."

The Chiefs led the NFL in yards and scoring during the regular season. Mahomes led the NFL in passing yards (5,250) and touchdown passes (41) and won the second MVP award of his career. He suffered a high-ankle sprain in the Chiefs' divisional round win against the Jaguars but played on it through the playoffs anyway, throwing for three touchdowns in the Super Bowl—two weeks after throwing two touchdowns and for more than 300 yards in the AFC Championship Game. "I wouldn't necessarily say we were counted out, but there were a lot more critics than there were the previous years I've been here," said Mahomes, who had taken note of the Chiefs' skeptics after the Hill trade. "At the beginning of the year, I said, 'As long as Andy Reid is coaching, we're going to have success as an offense.' And I was trusting the leaders that we have in that defense. So to go from a team—that I wouldn't even say a majority picked to win the AFC West, to win the Super Bowl—that speaks to the guys that we have in that locker room."

Other stars in the Chiefs' post-Hill world included, as always, Kelce, who seems to get better as the years pass. Even at the advanced football age of 33, Kelce had one of his best NFL seasons with 110 catches, 1,338 yards, and 12 touchdowns. He carried the Chiefs' offensively against the Jaguars after Mahomes' injury, recording 14 receptions and two touchdowns. "He's just smarter as a player," Mahomes said of Kelce's continued improvement. "That's the biggest thing. He knows how to get himself open. He knows how to use other people and other parts of the concept to get himself open and he's smart about how he blocks, how he can pin guys and get in the right position. He's just continued to evolve and be even better as a tight end. He is getting up there [in age]. I'm going to try to keep him here as long as possible, I promise you. He's not taking any screens like 80 yards anymore, I don't think. But he's still going to make some production on the field."

Even Kelce seemed impressed at what he was accomplishing. He referenced his game-winning touchdown against the Los Angeles Chargers in the final minute of Week 11. That 17-yard catch allowed the Chiefs to open a commanding lead in the AFC West race. Kelce lined up on the right side and then crossed the formation, running away from a top coverage safety, Derwin James. "I beat him with my legs, these 33-year-old legs," Kelce said afterward.

The Chiefs needed a big season from Kelce as much as—if not more than—ever after trading Hill. Kelce's initial concern after the trade about how the offense might operate and how effective he might be dissipated on the Chiefs' first drive of the season in the opening game against the Arizona Cardinals. Kelce scored the Chiefs' first touchdown on a nine-yard catch and later indicated the season energized him in a way he didn't fully expect. "I get excited for a new gameplan more than anything," Kelce said. "How are we going to attack these guys? How can I visualize how I'm going to attack my opponent all week long and all the various outcomes that could come on any given play? That's what you get fired up for."

In part because of the Hill trade, the Chiefs seem ready to sustain their success for the foreseeable future. They have stars like Mahomes, Kelce, and defensive tackle Chris Jones and now also a number of good young players to fill in around them. "Even though you may make moves and you may lose really good players, it doesn't mean there won't be a counterpunch and that we won't try to be aggressive in another way," Veach said. "What's needed to do that is draft resources and cap space. We're just going to find a new set of resources and try to be aggressive."

ACKNOWLEDGMENTS

No BOOK ABOUT THE CHIEFS would be complete without a tip of the hat to the Hunt family, which has been the steward of the franchise since its first season as the Dallas Texans of the American Football League in 1960. Franchise founder Lamar Hunt and—after his death in 2006—his son, Clark, have provided the type of stable leadership that any professional sports team would envy.

Lamar Hunt was never too busy to answer a question or simply talk football. He would always take a call or was quick to return a message when he couldn't. He saw that as part of his duty as the owner of Kansas City's football team. He was known to wander the parking lots at Arrowhead Stadium before games so he could tailgate with fans.

Clark's style is different than that of his father, but the role he's served for the football team has been no less important. I'll never forget an interview I did with him at the end of the 2007 season, his first full year as the team's chairman. We talked in his suite at Arrowhead, overlooking the snow-covered playing field. There was no need to clear the snow. The Chiefs had lost their last nine games, finished 4–12, and missed making the playoffs by a mile or more.

Hunt laid out in some detail that day the changes he would make in how the franchise operated. He held up the Pittsburgh Steelers, who rarely change head coaches and general managers, as the model.

I left that meeting thinking I didn't know how many Super Bowl championships the Chiefs would win with Clark Hunt as their owner, but that someday they would have a realistic chance.

It took longer than either of us thought for the Chiefs to get there. Hunt had to go through some growing pains and learn a few painful lessons about how to build a championship team. But I firmly believe the seeds for the Chiefs' 2019 Super Bowl championship team were planted in the visions he laid out that day.